THREE
PLAYS
OF RACINE

ANDROMACHE
BRITANNICUS
PHAEDRA

THREE
PLAYS
OF RACINE

TRANSLATED BY
GEORGE DILLON

THE UNIVERSITY OF CHICAGO PRESS

Library of Congress Catalog Card Number: 61-15938

THE UNIVERSITY OF CHICAGO PRESS, CHICAGO & LONDON
The University of Toronto Press, Toronto 5, Canada

© *1961 by The University of Chicago. Published 1961*
Composed and printed by THE UNIVERSITY OF CHICAGO
PRESS, *Chicago, Illinois, U.S.A.*

TO GLADYS CAMPBELL

"Que ne peut l'amitié . . . ?"

—RACINE

INTRODUCTION

Plays do not remain alive because their authors' names are illustrious or because their printed texts are important in the history of literature. They hold the stage because they hold audiences. In this respect Racine is the most remarkable writer of tragedies since Shakespeare; he has come to seem more and more remarkable as each hopeful new style of dramatic writing exposes its virtues and shortcomings. It is not that the various modern movements—romanticism, naturalism, symbolism, expressionism, and the rest—have failed to give us intensely interesting plays. But they have failed to give us one particular quality which tragedy of the first class provides.

Tragedy is concerned with violence and passion, but its effect is not to leave us shocked, angry, or sensually troubled. We are told that its original purpose was to cast out evil from the community. Yet it does not seek to minimize suffering and disaster or to explain them away. It rather proves them to be inevitable; it stresses the point by visiting them (always) on persons of the highest rank. At the same time it places them in the largest perspective and enables us in some way to see round them and be superior to them. It ends in a kind of exaltation.

The fact that audiences continue to respond to this quality suggests that, as playgoers if not as playwrights, we can still unquestioningly make the assumptions that underlie tragedy. Certainly we do make them while we are under the spell of a great tragic writer. We share his belief in the absolute worth and dignity of the individual, in the importance of an individual fate. We accept his view of humanity as a focus of superhuman interest. We do this the more easily because all good theater is a social experience, one that is peculiarly unhampered by time. In seeing or in imaginatively reading a great play, we become part of the original audience that made it possible; and through this audience we are united with a still older community, for whom tragedy and comedy were occasions of literal magic. The theater may become for us what it was in the beginning: a serious charm.

Yet it is not so much that a living play takes us into the past as that it brings various exciting elements of the past into the present. Racine, like any other dramatist, releases his full energy only in the here-and-now of actual performance—Racine particularly, for no playwright has ever been served by a more brilliant acting tradition. In reading him it is perhaps natural to visualize his men and women, not in an unearthly Greece or Rome or wherever they are supposed to be, but as they appear on the stage in distinct groups and pairs, standing at a hostile distance or drawn together by conspiracy or desire: poised but dynamic figures, moving in a severe décor but in the sumptuous and daring costumes that have always set off the French classical stage.

This is their special universe, stylized, almost abstract, meant to give only a poetic suggestion of time and place. Because of the formal language, the invincible *politesse*, it is always to some extent an idealization of the seventeenth-century French court. But at moments it can indeed also be Greece or Rome, as the dialogue echoes some phrase of Theocritus or the *Iliad*, some rhythmic effect of Virgil or bitter allusion of Tacitus. Racine candidly regales us with memories of everything that has ever appealed to him, including even the medieval court poetry that was scarcely recognizable as French. But all these borrowings are perfectly assimilated to his style. The scenes modeled on Greek plays have a disarming naturalness: he is concerned only with what delights him, not looking beyond the letter of the text for something ineffable or abstruse. He is, in his way, a shrewd and sensitive interpreter of the classics. He can bring them closer to us because he is aware of no distracting semantic barrier between the ancient writers and himself. And there is certainly none between his psychology and our own.

When he takes the *Hippolytus* of Euripides as a full-length model, using, as he says, "all that seemed to me most splendid" in it, one may think that on the contrary he ignores some of the chief splendors of that enigmatic and controversial play. Yet he makes of Phaedra's suffering a quite different and equally intense play, one that by virtue of its clarity is perhaps even more Greek. He belonged to an age that had the assurance to reject whatever seemed muddled or botched. Only in reading Scripture was it necessary, as Hobbes had said, "to captivate our understanding to the words." In the case of all other obscurities the reverse was true: they were to be "captivated" to common sense.

The enthusiasm of that age for neoclassical tragedy was obviously not a nostalgia for Orphic *logoi* or primordial rites. It was rather the pleasure of looking into a sublimating mirror. Since the time of Jodelle and Garnier, generations earlier, tragedies written on classical lines had been enjoying some literary success and had been performed in fashionable circles; but like the plays of Seneca, which most of them imitated, they had usually been given as dramatic readings before a small group. In the popular theater Alexandre Hardy, the playwright-manager whose troupe went barnstorming through the provinces, had employed classical elements in his pioneering tragicomedies. But now a new audience had grown up that permitted the commercial playhouses to offer, for the first time regularly in France, something more than the old unsophisticated and boisterous entertainments.

This audience, drawn largely from the rising middle class but governed by aristocratic tastes, was the substantial public which Molière called "the court and the town." It had made possible his comedies, as well as the tragedies of Corneille and Rotrou. Like Shakespeare's audience, though not so various, it represented a true community. It could enjoy the lightest distractions but it wanted also plays of a certain intellectual depth, which could reflect its own social, political, and philosophic interests. It wanted them in a form that would not invite suppression by the authorities.

No doubt the last thing anyone would have predicted before 1636 was a tragedy so stageworthy that it could fill a theater with two thousand persons and block several important streets with carriages and sedanchairs, for a long run. This phenomenon, the first of many, was *Le Cid*. It was not, to be sure, a Greek or Roman play: it had a medieval Spanish theme, but Corneille had written it in the grand style and, by dint of much effort, in the unitary classical form. It has rightly been called epoch-making. But the heyday of tragedy which it announced was only one aspect of an increasing general delight in all manner of impressive speech. By the time Racine established himself in Paris, twenty-six years later, people were reciting from memory even the plangent and frightening sermons of Bossuet. The great conversational salons, beginning with that of the Rambouillet palace, had become legendary in Europe. The young French Academy was busily drawing up a complete set of rules for grammar, rhetoric, and poetry. The celebration of language amounted to a new national *mystique*.

We are inclined to think of the century of Louis XIV as a baroque and worldly period. Racine himself remarked, in his youth, that it was a time when people were "vain of the slightest things"; and in his later years he wrote a great lyric poem "on the vain occupations of secular persons." But if it was a wordly time, it was also a thoughtful and even pious time—the piety often being the reaction from a lifetime of extreme worldliness. What was at first somewhat skeptically called "the current of piety" grew particularly strong in the last part of the century, until finally, under Madame de Maintenon's influence, it overtook even the king and the court. It overtook Racine at about the same time. The austere mood that had closed the English theaters for eighteen years, under the Cromwells, had not affected France during its worst religious and political strife, but eventually even the Paris theaters began to suffer from a new fashionable high-mindedness. Puritanical forces were already strong enough in 1664 to cause the banning of Molière's *Tartuffe* for five years.

Meanwhile a wonderful balance between high thinking and high living persisted. Outward display grew sumptuous: magnificent churches, palaces, esplanades appeared. Paris was taking on its final transcendent look. But the sinuous marvels of baroque art were not a native development; they were as foreign to the best French taste as the melodramatic pictures of Caravaggio's imitators that had been even longer in evidence. Baroque architecture was being gracefully adapted, but otherwise art in the true French spirit had little to do with all this. It had been finding its own way in the subtle but vigorous classical painting of Poussin and Claude Lorrain, and in the fresh realism of La Tour.

The whole baroque trend was originally part of the inspired showmanship of the Church of Rome in its efforts to counteract the Reformation. In France the spirit of excess was implemented by a new Bourbon king's anxiety to outdo the Hapsburgs, with their great imperial collections in Vienna, Madrid, Brussels, and (till the Swedish sacked it) Prague: as ruler of the new leading world power, Louis must not be accused of running a provincial court. So Bernini was brought from Rome and fêted, and an order given for quantities of his restless sculpture; but this was later withdrawn in deference to reviving classical taste. And while the king, disregarding his best counselors, was perfecting at Versailles the ultimate in extravagant palaces, the actual manners of his court were still to a large extent those of the old Louvre of Henri IV. There was a dwindling but substantial element, belonging to the tougher aristocracy, that would never frequent the grottoes fitted with boudoir cushions.

Certainly, as far as literature was concerned, the French seventeenth century was a *reaction* from the baroque. Poetry that may properly be called baroque, anticipating the English metaphysical style, had been written many years earlier—a poetry of some vigor and originality, but which has always been better liked by foreigners (including Milton and Goethe) than by the French. It was best exemplified by Du Bartas, who lived most of his short life before even Donne was born; it was briefly in competition with the romantic classicism of the Ronsard school. Ronsard had demonstrated the kind of lyric verve and imagination that we find in the Elizabethans, who admired and imitated him. It was in his time, if ever, that France might have produced something comparable to Elizabethan and Jacobean plays. But the French Renaissance style was never enriched with popular elements. The right theatrical conditions were lacking.

Malherbe, in any event, at the very turn of the century, had effectively ended the prestige of both schools. Malherbe wrote clear, vigorous, unimaginative poems that had the remarkable virtue of being truly lyrical in feeling though in most other respects more prosaic than most prose. His abstractness had become an ideal in all elevated language: truth was held to reside in the universal, not the particular. Since reason was believed to constitute truth, language must seek to be the exact reflection of thought. Therefore it must be purged of its sensuous dross: all images, ornaments, metaphors were to be avoided. This tendency was perhaps forwarded, in France as in England, by the new rationalizers of theology, who were concerned with putting an idea wherever there had formerly been a mental picture. In their view, it followed from man's godlike nature (they themselves would have said "deiform nature") that, as Basil Willey notes, "only the abstract, only what could be conceptually stated, could claim to be *real*: all else was shadow, image, or at least 'type' or symbol."

Such ideas became programmatic under the influence of such French critics and grammarians as Chapelain, and were soon extended to the theater, to enforce a separation of genres more uncompromising, if anything, than that observed by the Greeks. An intermediate style, called the *badinage noble,* was permitted to high comedy, but even Molière was criticized for sometimes falling below it, into the *bouffon.* In tragedy, of course, nothing but the sublime style would do. This was so limited and so abstract in its vocabulary and idiom that even Racine, to whom it was naturally congenial, sometimes complained of it bitterly. Writing about the *Odyssey,* he remarked that "words such as *calf* and *cows* are not shocking in Greek as they are in our language, which can scarcely tolerate anything."

At those moments when his poetic imagination did break through the abstract decorum to produce some concrete image, the result was so striking that the passage has usually become famous: for instance, his line about sowing the edge of precipices with flowers—*"Je leur semai de fleurs le bord des précipices"*—or, also from *Athalie*,[1] his twenty macabre lines describing the dream of Jezebel's disintegration, which Baudelaire, a hundred and sixty-six years later, would turn into his *Métamorphoses du Vampire*. Even Phaedra's complaint about her filleted hair, when it was first spoken from the stage of the Bourgogne, must have startled the very nymphs in the tapestries.

If the elevated language of the period had any exaggerated or baroque quality, it was this compulsive dignity, which could give a certain disdainful effect even to a lover's confession or an earnest prayer. The only fantasy it permitted itself was a run-down, rigidly codified set of euphemisms, known as the *langage de la galanterie*, which had survived in polite conversation from the preciosity of Ronsard's imitators, and which included all the accepted terms for sexual emotion and behavior. One of its most constant devices was that of summing up all a woman's attractions with some reference to her eyes: it was almost the only permissible compliment. The trials of love were represented by storms, iron bonds, arrows, prisons, and especially flames; indeed there are so many fires and flames in the writing of this period that it seems to have been the work of frustrated arsonists. It was part of Racine's originality that his characters could sometimes redeem such things by using them in deadly earnest, as when Phaedra speaks of being chased by the fires of Venus.

In the same way he made other conversational conventions, which he was obliged to use, yield unexpected value; even the proper names, those of his characters and of others who figure in their lives, are used as positive dramatic elements, for their suggestiveness and sonority. A particularly well-known line, sometimes called the most beautiful in French and cited as an illustration of "abstract" or "pure" poetry, is the one from *Phèdre* that combines two fabulous names: *"La fille de Minos et de Pasiphaé."* The names, the titles, the endless and indefeasible terms of address, the appeals to heaven, the diversity of moans, groans, sobs, hoots, shrieks, and rapturous cries permissively represented by the sign *"ah!"*—these, in Racine, are accessory, not fortuitous, elements, which

---

[1] In writing about Racine, I find it for some reason more natural to use the English form when referring to a character and the French form when mentioning a play-title. Sometimes, as in the case of *Britannicus*, they are the same.

enable the actors to pause, to vary their inflection, and in other ways to heighten their vocal interpretation as experience and intuition suggest.

Like every real playwright he had both the actor and the audience constantly in mind. Since equal persons of high rank could not, according to strict protocol, address each other by name, he let his royal characters very frequently use their privilege of referring to themselves in the third person; thus their identities remain clear even to forgetful or dim-sighted members of the audience. But all these histrionic devices are integrated into the poetry: the light way in which it carries its conventional elements is part of the highly co-ordinated effect of the French classical style.

"Equilibrium" is the usual word. It may be seen as the expression of a new hope and confidence that obtained for about thirty years in the latter part of the century. The king's effective reign, beginning with the death of Mazarin in 1661, was launched in an atmosphere of mutual forgiveness and trust. The civil disturbances of the Fronde were over, and a spirit of reconciliation had been growing for some years between partisans of the defiant great nobles and those of the royal power. It was that unprecedented moment, never to come again, when the French were weary of controversy. A phrase of Lucan was much quoted: *pacem summa tenent,* "There is peace on the heights."

This spirit had been greatly served by Corneille: his plays glowed with the dying individualism of Renaissance humanism, so that they appealed to the independent principles of the more stubborn aristocrats; but at the same time they showed apparently irreconcilable conflicts that were composed, after suitable bloodshed, by a change of heart in the antagonists. In the last act of *Cinna,* for example, one of his greatest plays, the five principal characters seem to be holding a contest in magnanimity. Such plays were enjoyed by the bourgeois and professional classes too, for the mood of willing submission to authority was now being reinforced by many social and economic opportunities. Louis believed in appointing capable bourgeois citizens to the highest posts. One of them, Colbert, a great national planner, was keeping employment high with his mercantile programs and building projects. Even the malversations of Fouquet, his predecessor, had been largely spent in patronizing cultural efforts, to the glory of France. And the generosity of the young king in such matters seemed to enhance his resemblance to Augustus, who had also brought despotism with peace.

All of this served to strengthen a deeper philosophic consensus, which had been defining itself for a generation and which had its mainstay in Descartes. He had seemed to demonstrate that reason and faith were mutually sustaining—good news indeed to minds troubled by the discrepancies between religion and science. No one could then foresee where the Cartesian method was actually leading: into the "chaos of clear ideas" that would call itself the Enlightenment, and toward a general lasting dissociation of truth and fact. For now that it was seen to be compatible with faith, reason had become a faith in itself. Only a few voices, notably Pascal's, had disputed its all-sufficiency, and these had impressed only a few minds of like persuasion, among them Racine's.

As the new sense of security found more and more complete expression in every genre of writing, the virtues of clarity, harmony, and proportion seemed to be permanent acquisitions. But the point of perfection is also the point of change. It is only a seeming paradox that the plays of Racine, which in every formal respect perfectly exemplify the rationalist ideal, were actually a profound challenge to the idolatry of reason.

Perhaps all that he was conscious of challenging, at least in the beginning, was the ascendancy of Corneille. This was at first a matter of technical strategy. Since the older poet could not be outdone in grandeur of rhetoric, Racine moved instinctively toward a simpler, more casual speech. He spaced his metrical pauses irregularly without violating the meter, alternated his periods with short sentences, used an occasional lively enjambment. He refrained from the antitheses and other sententious figures that had tended to weigh down the tragic style. Corneille was an excellent and inventive poet; he had inherited from Malherbe the ability to combine naturalness with formal correctness, and he had made the traditional French meter theatrically serviceable, giving it a *viva voce* drive. Racine went a step further. The audiences that thronged to *Andromaque* were struck particularly by the forthright quality of the dialogue: it seemed to them the most incisive language that had been heard in the theater. Racine achieved, at his best, an effect of spontaneity with precision.

This was acknowledged by some of Corneille's staunchest admirers, including Madame de Sévigné. What troubled them was that the change of tone involved something more than style. Racine's language, with its intimate and personal inflections, permitted an embarrassing candor: it seemed to operate on different levels, exposing not only the preoccupations of the rational and ethical mind but, almost at the same moment, the most dangerous promptings of the libido. Possibly the new rage for love novels, insipid as most of them were, had suggested to Racine the contemporary need for such expression, too long repressed by a rationalist literary discipline. Love, at any rate, became his characteristic theme—love in its full sexual urgency and usually in some neurotic and destructive form. It was a theme that enticed his imagination into the more somber realms of feminine psychology, enabling him to develop his unmerciful yet loving portraits of distracted women. These, more than any other accomplishment, would serve to make his reputation unique. Yet their perfection depended on all his skills.

Thus the break with Cornelian tragedy was clear cut. Love, in Corneille, was a constant element of drama, but it was expressed in conventional terms deriving from late-feudal literature; it was always chivalrous love, as unchangeable and unquestioned as the other duties and loyalties that motivated his characters. Corneille's characters could be great in wickedness as well as virtue, but the very language they used, which was in the grand epideictic tradition, made it impossible for them to admit any weakness. The audience knew from the start that they would surmount the most complicated problems—and often they were ludicrously complicated—or die in the attempt.

For a full generation these inspiring superegos had been parading across the stage, but it had long been apparent that they simply went round in a circle, reappearing in new costumes, and with each reappearance submitting themselves to a more critical scrutiny. There were those who had begun to ask of them, like Pericles seeing his daughter: "But are you flesh and blood? Have you a working pulse?" Racine, on the other hand, might give his audiences too little to admire, too few examples of sacrifice and spiritual triumph; the interest was likely to center in one of those appalling but strangely sympathetic women, at the expense of more virtuous sufferers. But though nothing else might work in the tortured lives of his characters, it was evident that their pulses did.

Corneille, himself an excellent critic, had said that his tragedies were based on the *pathétique d'admiration*. This, from the classical point of view, was a perfectly sound principle, going back to the ancient tomb ceremonies in honor of the great dead. As a single basis for tragedy, however, it was fairly limited. Most of Racine's plays could be deduced from an equally ancient and more mysterious rite, one that celebrated and sought to propitiate the darkest influences upon human destiny.

Racine let his characters make a shambles of every situation while trying earnestly to reason themselves out of their difficulties. In so doing he exposed the limitations of reason and offended the conservative minds of his day, but in so doing he was faithful to his understanding of tragedy. No playwright has more fully demonstrated the justice of Aristotle's observations on the subject; yet in answer to his critics he was usually content to quote one of them, pointing out that the tragic hero should have "a virtue capable of weakness." He might have replied with a still older Greek maxim: "Character is fate."

At the time of that great first success, *Andromaque*, the dramaturgy of fate must have been particularly evident to Racine in his own life. To be a playwright at all, he had had to endure the censure of those whom he deeply respected; yet it was perhaps the grounding they had given him in predestinarian concepts that enabled him to withstand their disapproval so long. The abbey of Port-Royal, just southwest of Paris, that exciting hotbed of Jansenism which had protected and appreciated his childhood, was in every affective sense his home. The great scholars who had taught him there, the nuns in their cream-colored habits sewn with the red cross, all the other friends he had made in that celebrated but persecuted institution—these were his true family. Undoubtedly he would have given his physical life for them. But now his life was in his talent: the theater challenged his intellect and stirred his orphan's desire to make a name in the world. Those who loved him had been forced to reprove him; and since he was their particular and precious responsibility, they had made the judgment severe. They had threatened him with excommunication and eternal fire.

At last he had inveighed against them in turn and now was desperately free; he would attempt to make a life in the fugitive world of the theater. A portrait in the Langres Museum, done probably at about the time of *Britannicus,* when he was thirty, suggests both the difficulty of that choice and the self-confidence it gave him. The large grey eyes have a kind of remorseful lucidity, but there is no remorse in the wilful, ironic mouth.

Yet the moral distress continued: its duration was exactly that of his fourteen years and ten plays in the theater, which were almost exactly in the middle of his life. Probably anyone inclined to do so could explain his choice of themes, characters, and situations, down to the last couplet, in terms of that central conflict. When it was finally resolved, in 1677, the crisis was so extreme that it has always been known as

Racine's conversion. He begged for permission to enter a Carthusian monastery, but his spiritual adviser was against it; "a Christian marriage" would be the right course for him—and it was. But perhaps the conflict could not have been resolved except that it had been so fully expressed in the plays, reaching its agony in Phaedra's lonely guilt, her sense of being an "outcast from all nature." At that point fate had had its way: his name was secure, his work irrevocably published. The two biblical tragedies, written more than a decade later and not even intended for the theater, were a kind of proud expiation.

Now fate makes his name ever more illustrious while keeping his work almost hermetically sealed in the French language, so that it is rather impertinent for a foreigner to discuss him at all. Yet it is customary for persons writing about him in English to make some attempt to estimate his merits in comparison with those of Shakespeare. This is like trying to decide between a Greek temple and the Milan cathedral —an unreal problem, for when we are in the mood to be strongly impressed by one we are likely to be somewhat insensitive to the charms of the other. But there is no reason why we cannot enjoy both writers on different occasions; and in turning from one to the other we may find our perception heightened by the total contrast. Certainly our appreciation of their originality will be increased.

The great copious texts of Shakespeare must be reduced to acting versions in the theater—hundreds of different versions—at the discretion of stars and directors, but their profusion does not embarrass us in print. Shakespeare's excursive plotting, suited to his more popular audience and the conditions of his theater, actually released his imagination and gave it necessary scope; he was always concerned, not merely with telling a story, but with communicating the sense of a multifarious, surprising world. But in this as in so much else, Shakespeare is alone: no other writer for the stage has made such a virtue of abundance. What we most *often* enjoy in the theater is the tightly constructed Racinian plot showing a single action, usually near its climax when the play begins, of which the earlier developments are explained to us through one or another retrospective device. Every new play of this type, whether its setting is Athens, London, Greenwich Village, or Mississippi, is directly descended from Racine. So are all our novels of the more compressed sort, which confine the narrative to a short dramatic continuum and bring past events to light through the characters' speech and thoughts: their line goes back to *La Princesse de Clèves,* which was noticeably influenced by Racine. Madame de La Fayette and La Roche-foucauld were writing it during the first Paris run of *Phèdre.*

When we compare the apparently effortless simplicity of *Andro-maque* or any other Racine play with some of the strained plotting and crude scene transitions of his contemporaries, we realize that this archi-tectonic sense was something new in the modern theater, an illustra-tion of Picasso's dictum that "technique is what is not learned." In Racine the exposition is woven through the whole text of a play, and the most important facts are repeated until we cannot forget them; every good playwright does this, but the exceptional thing is that none of this background material seems to be imparted for our information, or even particularly for the benefit of the person addressed, but rather for the satisfaction and relief of the person speaking—to give vent to his fears or doubts, to analyze a problem, to review a menacing train of events, and so on. Everything is a dramatic opportunity.

Of course the most brilliant opportunities, of which at least one is given to every principal actor, are the *tirades.* Their chief purpose is not to wrap up great masses of exposition or otherwise to substitute for the Greek prologues and choruses; they often do this, it is true, but Racine was quite capable of doing it in less obvious ways. Their special value is to *fix* attention on each personage for a few moments, giving us an im-pression of his character in full relief, against the background of his relevant past. In *Andromaque,* for example, Orestes' first long speech is not simply an account of what has happened during the preceding six months—this could have been given to us piecemeal throughout the first act or two—but primarily the expression of his own passionate, sincere, unbalanced nature.

Or again, the long speech may have exactly the same purpose as that of the Greek messenger, in which case it may be given to a secondary character. It then serves to describe a violent action and to bring its pathos home to us more deeply than if we saw it shammed on the stage. But first, last, always, each one of these *tirades* (the French word has no implication of rant) is a means of realizing the highest potential of the actor. Racine knew that the actor, in his personal magnetism and instinctive art, is the basis of all theater, what audiences really come to see. The very long speeches would be tedious only if they were tediously read. In reading them to ourselves it is necessary to imagine what an actual or ideal performer would do with them. We then see

how much they enable him to do, and that, far from being fits of gar-
rulity, they are often marvelously compact.

But what of the language as poetry, when we encounter it in the
hard glare of the printed page?

It must be admitted that, for us who have been brought up on Shakespeare, Racine's dialogue may at first seem coldly conventional. This
is not only due to the absence of colorful tropes, images, and idioms, but
to the meter itself; the alexandrine, especially in a long composition,
seems to us much less natural than it does to a French reader. We are
always conscious of the ingenious versification: each line of exactly
twelve syllables divided by a central caesura, which may be a distinct
or an almost imperceptible pause, the resulting halves being often themselves divided, the vowel quantities (a life-and-death matter in French)
precisely grouped and balanced, the couplets ending alternately in
masculine and feminine rhymes.

All these things, we know, have a purely phonetic bearing. They enable the prosody to define itself in spite of the constant shifting of stress;
they enable the ear to keep its place, so to speak, in the absence of a
fixed tonic accent or of any accentual scheme. Yet, fascinated by their
intricacy, reading mainly with the eye, we are aware of the strictness of
the form rather than the endless rhythmic variation that occurs within
the form. We find it hard to believe that this severely stylized poetry
should have caused so many women to faint in Racine's contemporary
audiences, or that the exertions demanded by Orestes' delirium—surely
the most urbane of mad scenes—could have brought on the death of
Montfleury, who created the part.

Then we hear it properly spoken, and we realize that the strict form
of this language is one of its most practical qualities. It is, in the highest
degree, that "co-presence of something regular" which, as Wordsworth
said, is needed to control and direct the emotions aroused by tragedy
and by the most intense comedy; it is a means of sustaining the lively
but equable tone of the play. We discover, too, that it in no way inter-
feres with the communication of feeling. The emotion proper to each
speech is inherent in the very sound of the poetry—inherent but un-
insistent. It waits for the actor to heighten and project it.

This reticence is at the opposite extreme from Elizabethan dialogue,
in which the most casual emotions are asserted, elaborated, demonstrated,
and exploited by every resource of language. In Shakespeare the language *is* the drama. In his greatest scenes the verbal magnificence tends

to overmatch even the best players, so that we can seldom listen to those scenes without a nervous longing to reread the text, to recover what has been diminished or marred. Racine cannot give us the faintest hint of that magnificence. He was deprived, quite willingly, of the incomparable richness of idiom that resulted from mixing the high and the low styles, and of all the other "barbarous advantages," as Goethe called them, which Shakespeare turned to account.

On the other hand, as formal and abstract as it is, Racine's poetry is more consistently functional in the theater. It was written to serve the actor, not to compete with him or to compensate for him. Demanding of him strict verbal fidelity, including metrical fidelity, but relying at every point on his special skills, it gives him great latitude to develop his own interpretation. How great this is may be judged from the accounts of many celebrated performances. Describing Sarah Bernhardt as Phaedra, Arthur Symons wrote: "She seems to abandon herself wholly, at times, to her *fureurs;* she tears the words with her teeth and spits them out of her mouth, like a wild beast ravening upon its prey; but there is always dignity, restraint, a certain remoteness of soul, and there is always the verse, and her miraculous rendering of the verse . . . everything is colored by the poetry, everything is subordinate to beauty."

Racine is a translatable poet only in the most limited sense. Even his English contemporaries, who greatly admired him, were able to evoke only a demure specter of his style. But a translation can show his concentrated dramatic method; it can show the fulness, and something of the force, of his characterization. I believe it can do this best, for some readers, by following his vocabulary and basic sentence structure as closely as possible, rather than by trying, at all costs, for a sustained musical effect. I have thought, too, that there should be at least one Racine translation showing all the speeches in their original length, so that the whole carefully adjusted time scheme of the play would not be lost.

No English meter can suggest the spoken quality of Racinian verse—least of all, in extended use, the one that superficially resembles it, a succession of rhymed couplets. The alexandrines fall as naturally on French ears as everyday conversation, for in French it is almost easier to rhyme than not to rhyme: an audience listening to Racine would become aware of the rhyme or the caesura only if one or the other were lacking. This is as true today as it must have been in the 1660's. Yet the noble music has its part in the dramatic effect; it is like that of the most skilful instrumental accompaniment to a film, but even more essential. In contrast, the traditional verse of our own theater, unrhymed pentameter, quickly becomes obtrusive, as obtrusive as English rhyme, when it falls into syllabic regularity. It has to be varied, and it permits so much variety that it can even accommodate prose. But it is still, for dramatic purposes, our meter most nearly equivalent to that of Racine.

The three plays I have chosen are those that have had the greatest long-term success both with audiences and with critics—no doubt because they introduce Racine's three most remarkable women characters: Phaedra, Hermione, and Agrippina. Of course they have been the most often translated. Those translations that have attempted to be most literal are unfortunately those with the most glaring inaccuracies. But they are seldom readable. The best-known English versions are those of R. B. Boswell, brought out in London in 1889–90. They have sometimes been reprinted, with minor revisions, under other names. Boswell is literal when it suits his convenience; he knows exactly what he is about, and he communicates his sense of Racine's directness and simplicity. His occasional wild misrenderings simply prove that he worked from a faulty text.

Since then we have had the highly finished translations of Mr. Lacy Lockert. Done in rhyme, they resort even more freely to paraphrase but show a perfect grasp of the original in all its implications and allusions. There have also been some interesting versions of single plays, from Thomas Otway's contemporary imitation of *Bérénice* to Mr. Robert Lowell's recent adaptation of *Phèdre*. This last, the freest of all, has the authority of an original work; in its imaginative power and great nervous vitality it seems almost to create a new genre. My own intention has been something different from all of these and perhaps supplementary to them: a line-for-line translation that would be as *literal* as differences in idiom permit.

I am most grateful to Alix du Poy for her many shrewd and enlivening criticisms; and I am conscious, as always, of my indebtedness to the John Simon Guggenheim Memorial Foundation for the inestimable gift, made to me almost thirty years ago, of two years of carefree study in France.

GEORGE DILLON

ANDROMACHE

This play, the third of Racine's tragedies, was first given before the court at Versailles, in the Queen's apartments, November 17, 1667; it opened the next day in Paris, in the venerable Bourgogne palace, where the company of actors had their theater. It was a brilliant and disturbing success. Racine, then not quite twenty-eight, having all but forfeited his deepest attachments to pursue the dream of fame, had suddenly to cope with the reality: he became at once a target for the strenuous criticism which he always found difficult. Until then he had been just one of several followers in the steps of Corneille; his *Thébaïde* and his *Alexandre,* mildly praised for their versification but blamed for coldness, had been little discussed. With *Andromaque* he incurred the sincere disapproval of many of the old guard who swore by Corneille, as well as the hatred of various lesser writers and their resourceful cliques. They could no longer regard him as a talented upstart who had had some personal success at court. He had launched what was to be known for two generations as "the new tragedy."

What was its novelty? Most obviously it was the emphasis placed on love in its more violent aspects: in this play, the power of indifference and cruelty, not to subdue, but greatly to heighten, sexual desire. It was also the more direct language and the uncontrived plots. But perhaps essentially it was the fact that most of the characters bring disaster upon themselves while laying the shrewdest and most resolute plans to avoid it. They act, in the end, against their better judgment. In *Andromaque,*

1

for example, Hermione and Orestes have learned to read each other like a book, yet each finally misjudges the other's sincerity. This was a radical departure from the heroic Cornelian play; and though no one from the pit to the gallery could doubt, emotionally, that it was true to life, the typical seventeenth-century morality, which equated reason and nature, was bound to take another look. Such a view of humanity was unedifying. It had its place in comedy, but classical tragedy was supposed to exemplify the highest virtues of *les âmes bien nées,* as the master himself had said. The most prominent criticism of *Andromaque,* that of Subligny, complained that none of the characters were noble enough. Not even the engaging Pylades. Not even Andromache, who might almost have been drawn by Corneille: she was reproached for lack of self-possession and prudence.

Racine, in his preface to the published text, quoted a few lines from the *Aeneid* (iii. 292 ff.) and said that this passage contained "the whole subject" of his play. It is the part where Hector's widow, the captive princess Andromache, brings offerings to the symbolic tomb—a mound of green turf between two altars—she has dedicated to Hector in Epirus. She laments that, instead of being killed at Troy, she has been spared to endure the lust of Pyrrhus; but she observes that Orestes, "driven by the Furies of his crimes," has punished Pyrrhus for robbing him of Hermione. Certain other details came from the *Iliad,* from Euripides' *Andromache,* and from Seneca's *Trojan Women.* But Racine, with his dependable flair for a good story, made one important change: when the play opens, his heroine has not been violated by Pyrrhus. We are presented, not with the ravishment of Hector's wife by her captor, but with something far more dramatic—her attempted seduction.

The handling of this variation, with its emphasis on Andromache's inconsolability, seems to point to another, perhaps unconscious, literary source: the ancient shocker known as *The Widow Who Was Comforted.* This Milesian fable may well have been one of those Greek novels that were thrown in the fire when Racine, as a youth, was caught reading them at Port-Royal. In all its adaptations—whether it becomes, as in Petronius, merely a ribald anecdote, or, as in D. H. Lawrence, a solemn but indecorous romance-with-a-thesis—the undying plot retains a certain ironic suspense. Here it is in the nature of a vague suggestion: we do not really expect Andromache to go from one extreme to the other, but the fact that her situation holds such a possibility is enough to sustain interest through the critical first act. Afterward the play is almost continuously stolen by Hermione, a development that may have astonished Racine himself. This unbridled young egoist was his first attractive horror —a character whom we take pleasure in hating but, because she is so ingenuous and so deeply hurt, nevertheless forgive.

Meanwhile the slight uncertainty about Andromache continues to be an element of suspense; in his concern to maintain it Racine perfected the wholly original and lifelike quality that is always spoken of in connection with this character, her *coquetterie vertueuse*. It was not a superficial device. The early criticisms are more understandable when we consider that in the first acted and published version she reappeared at the end of the play, to express her feeling that, because of what he has suffered for her, Pyrrhus indeed "seems to have taken my Hector's place." This was rightly omitted—much better to let Andromache keep her secret—but it shows that in Racine's mind she was not made of Trojan bronze.

In Corneille the characters were at odds with one another, but never, or only for a fleeting moment, with themselves. They might be torn between conflicting duties and loyalties, but these were rarely self-imposed and hardly questioned; unless something very fortunate happened, death was to be sought as the one honorable way out. The monolithic integrity of these "well-born souls," inspiring as it often was, tended to make of them almost another species; and the situations, though cast on the psychological plane, tended to be static. They could be developed only under the pressure of circumstances, so that something fortuitous and melodramatic was often needed to resolve them. In *Andromaque* the important conflicts are primarily within, only by extension between, the characters. The action moves forward inevitably, of itself, as all but Andromache commit a fatal sequence of errors due to their illusions about themselves and one another, or, betrayed by passion, suddenly shift their course. They do it for the most part unconsciously, or at least against their wills, while analyzing every situation in what seems to them the most lucid way.

Racine's admirers, theorizing about tragedy, were quite ready to show that this was "good Aristotle." Nevertheless it was heresy to the age of reason. It looked forward, and back, to an insight belonging to less confident times: it regarded intellect as the slave of the passions. The lifelong partisans of Corneille felt it to be subversive and they were right. The post-Renaissance twilight had deepened.

CHARACTERS

Andromache
Widow of Hector and captive of Pyrrhus

Pyrrhus
Son of Achilles and king of Epirus

Orestes
Son of Agamemnon

Hermione
Daughter of Helen; engaged to Pyrrhus

Pylades
Friend of Orestes

Cleone
Confidante of Hermione

Cephissa
Confidante of Andromache

Phoenix
Tutor of Pyrrhus, formerly of Achilles

Soldiers of Orestes' suite

The scene is at Buthrotum, a city of Epirus, in a hall
of the palace of Pyrrhus

ACT ONE

(*Enter Orestes and Pylades.*)

Orestes

    Yes, now that I recover so true a friend,
    my fortune wears a new face; it would seem
    already to have tempered its savagery
    since it rejoins us here. Who would have said
    that a seacoast so grim to my desires   5
    would, on the instant, present Pylades
    to Orestes' eyes—you, more than six months lost,
    at the court of Pyrrhus be restored to me?

Pylades

    I thank heaven, which, continually delaying,
    seemed to have closed to me the way to Greece   10
    after the fatal day when, with Epirus
    almost in view, the storm parted our ships.
    What dark thoughts I have had, here in this exile,
    what deep regret for your misfortunes, fearing
    always for you some dangerous new plight   15
    my troubled friendship had no way to share.
    I dreaded, above all, that melancholy
    in which so long I watched you bury alive
    your soul: I feared heaven, by a cruel favor,
    would offer you the death you still pursued.   20
    But now, my lord, I see you; and dare I say
    a happier fate has led you to Epirus?
    The pomp that trails you here is not, indeed,
    that of a luckless wretch who comes to die.

Orestes

    Alas, who knows the destiny that brings me?   25
    Love brings me, seeking a cruel girl; but all
    it may decide against my fate, who knows,
    or whether I come seeking life or death?

Pylades

    What, is it true? Your soul a slave to love,
    you are thrown upon its mercy? By what charm,   30
    forgetting so much agony endured,
    could you consent to wear those irons again?
    Do you suppose Hermione, cold in Sparta,
    waits burning in Epirus? Well ashamed
    to have persisted in such useless prayers,   35
    you hated her, you spoke no more of her.
    Sir, you deceived me.

Orestes

                  I deceived myself.
    Friend, do not put to scorn an unhappy man
    who loves you: have I ever hidden from you
    my heart, my hopes? You knew my first desire;   40
    at last, when Menelaus pledged his daughter
    to Pyrrhus, avenger of his family,
    you saw my hopelessness; and, since, you have watched me
    dragging the weight of it from sea to sea.
    I saw you with regret, in that dismal state,   45
    ready to follow the poor, wronged Orestes
    no matter where—alert to check my violence,
    and, indeed, save me constantly from myself.
    But when, among those dangers, I recalled
    Hermione lavishing herself on Pyrrhus,   50
    you know in what a lively rage my heart
    willed, by forgetting, to requite her scorn.
    I made believe, I did believe, I had won.
    I took my frenzied moods for hate. Detesting
    her cruelty, belittling her attractions,   55
    I dared her eyes to trouble me again.
    And so I thought to stifle my tenderness.
    In that deceptive calm I arrived in Greece,
    to find its princes gathered that very day,
    troubled, it seemed, by some quite urgent peril.   60
    I ran to it. War and its triumphs, I thought,
    would give me grander cares to reflect upon,
    my senses be restored to their first keenness,
    and love be driven from my heart. But now

wonder with me at fate, which sends me running,   65
even then, pell-mell into the hated trap.
I hear, on all sides, murmuring against Pyrrhus;
all Greece complains: the plaint is that, forgetting
his promise and his ancestry, he rears
within his court the enemy of Greece,   70
Astyanax, Hector's young ill-fated son,
heir of so many dead kings under Troy.
I hear, to snatch his infancy from the sword,
Andromache deceived the astute Ulysses,
that, wrested from her arms, another child   75
under her son's name went to death. They say,
indifferent to Hermione, my rival
Offers in a new quarter his heart and crown.
Though not believing it, Menelaus looks sad
and grumbles about a wedding so long put off.   80
Among the cares in which his soul is drowned,
a secret joy rises in mine: I triumph;
and still, at first, I wish to imagine it
the exciting taste of vengeance. But too soon
the thankless woman ruled again in my heart.   85
I knew again the torturing hot coals
of ill-suppressed desire; I felt my hate
was dying. Rather, I knew I loved her still.
So I invite the suffrage of all Greeks.
I am sent to Pyrrhus; I undertake this voyage.   90
I come to see if one can wrest from him
that child whose life disturbs so many States:
most fortunate, in my impatient ardor,
if I could seize, not Astyanax but my princess!
For do not think my passion, now doubly strong,   95
will flinch at the worst dangers. Knowing too well,
after such efforts, all resistance vain,
I accept blindly its fatal urging. I love:
I am here to seek Hermione—to win her,
to escape with her, or perish before her eyes.   100
You know Pyrrhus. What do you think he will do?
Give me the present drift of his court, his heart.
Does my Hermione still rule him? Will he
return to me, Pylades, what he has stolen?

Pylades

 I should be false, my lord, if I promised you   105
 that he would place her willingly in your hands.
 Not that he seems to enjoy his conquest. He burns
 with a most obvious fire for Hector's widow;
 he loves her: but that unyielding widow till now
 has given him, in return, but hatred; and still   110
 one sees him, every day, try every means
 to touch his captive's heart, or terrify her.
 He threatens her son's life, whom he keeps hidden,
 starts her tears flowing, then at once relents.
 Hermione herself a hundred times   115
 has seen this angry lover return to her
 and swear obedience, offering at her feet
 his tortured promise, less in love than rage.
 Do not hope, then, to know the present will
 of a heart that rules itself so little: he could—   120
 my lord, he could, in this confusion, marry
 the one he hates, and send his love to death.

Orestes

 But tell me in what light Hermione sees
 her beauty ineffective, her marriage postponed.

Pylades

 Hermione, sir, at least in outward show,   125
 seems to disdain her lover's inconstancy.
 She thinks he will come, relieved to win forgiveness,
 begging her to command his heart again.
 But she has shown me, in confidence, her tears:
 she weeps for the insult to her charms. Forever   130
 at the point of leaving, forever staying on,
 she calls, at times, Orestes to her aid.

Orestes

 Oh, if I thought so, Pylades, I would go
 fling myself now—

Pylades

     My lord, complete your mission.
 You await the King: speak out and let him see   135
 all Greeks united against Hector's son.
 Far from abandoning that son of his darling,

he will love better for their hate. The more
one tries to part them, the closer they'll be bound.
Press hard: ask everything, to obtain nothing.   140
 He is here.
Orestes
            Go, then, dispose the cruel one
to see a lover who comes for her alone.
                 (*Exit Pylades. Enter Pyrrhus and Phoenix.*)
Before the Greeks, with one voice, speak through me,
let me say here I am honored by their choice,
and express some happiness, my lord, at seeing   145
Achilles' son, Troy's conqueror. Your deeds
move us to wonder as your father's did.
Hector went down before him, Troy before you;
 and by a fine audacity you have proved
none but Achilles' son could take his place.   150
But now we see you—this he would not have done—
help to revive the evil of Trojan blood,
and, touched by a fatal pity, give asylum
to the last relic of those years of strife.
My lord, do you not recall what Hector was?   155
Our weakened populations remember still.
Our widows and daughters tremble at his name.
There is no family in all Greece but asks
retaliation upon that hapless son
for husband or for parent lost to Hector.   160
Who knows what he may undertake one day?
Perhaps we shall see him, like his father, thrust
into our ports to set our ships alight
and, flame in hand, pursue them across the water.
My lord, may I tell you what I think? Even you   165
foresee with fear the wages of your good deed,
knowing this serpent strengthened in your bosom
may punish you, one day, for having spared him.
Yield, then, to all the Greeks. Assure their vengeance,
assure your life: cast out an enemy,   170
one the more dangerous that he will try
first upon you the war he means for them

9

Pyrrhus

    Greece is too much concerned in my behalf:
    I thought her agitated by graver cares;
    the name of her ambassador, my lord,   175
    made me conceive more grandeur in her designs.
    Who would think, truly, such a task deserved
    the mediation of Agamemnon's son;
    that a whole people, after so many triumphs,
    would scheme no better thing than a child's death?   180
    To whom, then, am I charged to sacrifice him?
    Does Greece retain some warrant upon his life?
    May I alone, of all Greeks, not dispose
    of a captive fate has dealt me? For so it was,
    my lord, when under the smoking walls of Troy   185
    the victors, dark with blood, divided their prey:
    chance, whose decrees were then observed, let fall
    into my hands Andromache and her son.
    Hecuba perished near Ulysses; Cassandra
    was led to Argos by your father. To these,   190
    to their prisoners, have I extended my claims?
    Have I had any profit from their exploits?
    It is feared that Troy, with Hector, will revive,
    his son repay me death for life. My lord,
    so much foreknowledge brings too much unease: 195
    I cannot see disasters so far off.
    I think what formerly that city was,
    so proud in ramparts, so profuse in heroes,
    Mistress of Asia; then I bring to mind
    Troy's fate, and what she is today. I see   200
    only a cluster of cinder-blackened towers,
    a river stained with blood, some deserted fields,
    a child held captive; and I cannot think
    Troy, in this state, aspires to vengeance. Why,
    if the destruction of Hector's son was sworn,   205
    have we waited a full year? Why was he not
    immolated in Priam's arms and left
    under the mass of slaughtered, under Troy?
    All was fair, then: old age and smallest childhood
    relied in vain for mercy upon their weakness;   210

the victory and the night, more cruel than we,
excited us to murder, sent wild our blows.
My rage was but too fierce toward the conquered ones.
But that my cruelty should survive my anger,
that, though my heart is clutched by pity, my hands   215
should bathe deliberately in a child's blood?
No, my lord; let the Greeks find other prey,
let them seek elsewhere what remains of Troy.
My enmities have run their course; Epirus
shall be the guardian of what Troy has saved.   220

Orestes

My lord, you know too well by what artifice
a false Astyanax was put to death,
when only the son of Hector should have died;
Hector, not Troy, is the quarry. Yes, the Greeks,
in striking at the son, pursue the father;   225
their anger has been purchased with too much blood.
It cannot die but in his own. Even here,
to Epirus, the hatred of that blood may draw them:
prevent them.

Pyrrhus

           Not at all. I am very willing.
Let them seek Epirus a second Troy;   230
let them, in muddled fury, no longer know
the blood that made them conquer from that of the conquered.
But then it is nothing new, that Greece rewards
the service of Achilles with injustice.
Hector profited by it, and some day   235
his son, my lord, could profit in his turn.

Orestes

So Greece, in you, finds a rebellious child?

Pyrrhus

Was I the conqueror, only to be her subject?

Orestes

Hermione, my lord, will check your boldness:
her eyes will come between her father and you.   240

Pyrrhus

Hermione, my lord, I may still hold dear
without becoming her father's slave. Perhaps

I shall some day have the skill to reconcile
my royal obligations and those of my love.
You may, however, see the daughter of Helen: 245
I know how close the ties of blood between you.
Thereafter I shall not detain you, my lord,
and you may take my refusal to the Greeks.

(Exit Orestes.)

Phoenix
And so you send him to the feet of his love?
Pyrrhus
He has burned, they say, a long time for the princess.   250
Phoenix
But if that flame, my lord, should be revived?
If he gave back his heart and made her love him?
Pyrrhus
Let them love, Phoenix. I grant it. Let her go:
let them return in mutual ravishment
to Sparta. All our ports are open to them.   255
How much she would save me of constraint and care!
Phoenix
My lord—
Pyrrhus
                Another time I will tell you all.
Andromache is here.

(Enter Andromache and Cephissa. Exit Phoenix.)
                Madam, you sought me?
Have I the right to such a charming hope?
Andromache
I was going to the place where they keep my son.   260
Since you permit me once a day to see
all I have left of Hector and of Troy,
I was going, my lord, to weep with him a moment:
I have not held him in my arms today.
Pyrrhus
Madam, the Greeks, to judge by their alarm,   265
will give you soon some further cause to weep.
Andromache
And what can be the present fear, my lord,
that strikes their hearts? Did any Trojan escape you?

12

Pyrrhus
    Their anger against Hector is not appeased:
    they fear his son.   270
Andromache
                    How worthy of their fear,
    a suffering child who does not yet know Pyrrhus
    his master, or himself the son of Hector!
Pyrrhus
    Such as he is, all Greece demands his death.
    The son of Agamemnon is here to urge it.
Andromache
    And you will give so barbarous a command?   275
    Is it on my account that he is guilty?
    They do not fear he will avenge his father,
    alas! They fear he will console his mother.
    He would have taken a father's, a husband's, place;
    but all must go, and always by your hand.   280
Pyrrhus
    Madam, I have refused them, to spare your tears.
    The Greeks have threatened me with force; but though
    they should return across the waters to claim
    your son with a thousand ships, though it should require
    all the blood Helen set flowing, though I myself   285
    should see, after ten years, my palace in ashes,
    I do not falter, I take his part at once.
    I will defend his life at cost of mine.
    But, among these dangers I invite to please you,
    will you refuse me a less hostile look?   290
    Hated by all the Greeks, pressed on all sides,
    must I withstand your cruelties as well?
    My arm is raised in your service. May I hope
    you will accept a heart, too, that adores you?
    Doing battle for your sake, may I believe   295
    you are not numbered among my enemies?
Andromache
    My lord, what are you saying? What will Greece say?
    Should such a noble heart betray such weakness?
    Would you have so good, so generous a design
    pass for a lover's exaltation? Captive,   300

forever joyless, wearisome to myself,
how can you wish Andromache to love you?
What charms for you have these ill-fated eyes
you have sentenced to perpetual tears? No, no,
respect the plight of an adversary, save   305
two helpless beings, restore a son to his mother,
oppose the cruelty of a hundred tribes,
without requiring my heart in payment. Shield him,
if he is threatened, in spite of me: my lord,
that would be worthy of Achilles' son.   310

Pyrrhus

So your anger has not lived its time? Can one
hate constantly and never fail to punish?
I have made some grieve, no doubt. In Phrygia, too,
my hand was reddened with the blood of your race
a hundred times. But how your eyes have moved me!   315
How costly to myself the tears they have shed,
how much remorse they have given me! I endure
all the calamities I wreaked at Troy:
conquered, in irons, consumed by penitence,
burned with more fires than I have ever lit—   320
such wakefulness, such tears, such long desire . . .
was I ever as cruel as you? But now enough
of punishing and being punished in turn;
the enemies we have in common should bind us
in one cause. Madam, tell me only to hope: 325
I give you back your son and serve as his father;
I will teach him to avenge Troy; I will go
and scourge the Greeks for your afflictions and mine.
Excited by one look, I can venture all:
your Ilium can rise again from its ashes;   330
more quickly than it was taken by the Greeks,
within its risen walls I can crown your son.

Andromache

My lord, such grandeurs hardly touch us now:
I promised them to him while his father lived.
But no, you do not hope to see us again,   335
sacred walls, which my Hector could not save!
The unfortunate pretend to smaller favors,

14

my lord; it is an exile my tears demand.
Far from the Greeks and even from yourself,
let me go hide my son and mourn my husband.   340
Your love sets burning too much hate against us:
return, return to the daughter of Helen.
Pyrrhus

                                        Madam,
can I do this? Ah, how you torture me!
How shall I give her back a heart you hold?
I know she was promised all my love and duty;   345
I know she came to Epirus to wear the crown;
you were led here by fate, the one and the other,
you a chained captive, she to impose her chains.
But have I been concerned with her happiness?
Would one not say, seeing the contrary,   350
your charms all-powerful and hers rejected,
that she is prisoner here, and that you reign?
Why, if one sigh of all I breathe for you
were given for her, she would be greatly cheered.
Andromache

And why would she be hostile to your sighs?   355
Has she forgotten your past services?
Does Troy, does Hector, make her being revolt
against you? Is she sworn to a husband's ashes?
And what a husband! Deep-wounding memory!
Only his death has made your sire immortal: 360
the brightness of his sword is but Hector's blood,
and you would both be nameless but for my tears.
Pyrrhus

Well, madam, have it so. I must obey:
I must forget you, or more justly, hate you.
Yes, my desires have run too wildly on   365
to find repose, now, in mere unconcern.
Look to it well: from this time forward my heart,
if it cannot love with rapture, must hate with fury.
I will spare nothing in my lawful rage:
the son will answer for the mother's contempt;   370
Greece wants it; and I will not risk forever
my good name to defend ingratitude.

Andromache

    Alas, he will die, then. He has no defense
    but his mother's tears and his innocence. Perhaps,
    at this late hour and in my present state,   375
    his death will bring the end of my torture near.
    I prolonged life and suffering for him,
    but, following him, I shall rejoin his father.
    So, my lord, by your efforts reunited,
    we shall all three—   380

Pyrrhus

              Go, madam, see your son.
    In seeing him, your love may be less bold,
    less willing to take anger for its guide.
    Soon I shall join you, to know our destinies:
    madam, embracing him, take thought to save him.

ACT TWO

(*Enter Hermione and Cleone.*)

Hermione

I am doing what you wish: I shall let him see me;   385
I do consent to give him that joy again.
In a moment Pylades will bring him here;
but if I obeyed myself, I should not see him.

Cleone

And what is dreadful to you about his sight?
Madam, is he not still the same Orestes   390
for whose return you have wished a hundred times,
whose constancy and love you have regretted?

Hermione

That love too thanklessly repaid—it is this
that makes his presence here so difficult.
What shame for me, what triumph for him, to see   395
my disappointment equal his own chagrin!
Is this, he will say, that proud Hermione?
She scorned me; now another abandons her.
That cold heart, which she held at such a price,
is learning, then, in turn, to endure contempt?   400
Ah, Gods!

Cleone

                Oh, banish these unworthy fears!
He has been charmed too well. Do you suppose
a lover journeys here to bring you insults?
He brings a heart he could not keep from you.
But you say nothing of what a father writes.   405

Hermione

If Pyrrhus is inclined to delay further,
if he will not consent to the Trojan's death,
my father orders me to sail with the Greeks.

Cleone

Why, then, my lady, listen to Orestes.

17

Pyrrhus began it: now, at least, finish it.   410
To do it well, act before he decides.
Have you not told me you hated him?
Hermione

                           Do I hate him,
Cleone! The honor of my name is at stake,
after the host of favors he has forgotten.
He whom I held so dear, who could still betray me!   415
Ah, I have loved too deeply, not to hate.
Cleone

Then leave him, madam; and since you are adored—
Hermione

No, give my fury time to grow! I would be
more surely armed against my adversary:
Cleone, I wish to turn from him in horror.   420
He will help me, all too well, the faithless one!
Cleone

What! Are you waiting for some new affront?
To love a captive, and love her before your eyes,
this has not made him hateful? After this,
what else could he imagine? You would be   425
offended now, if he could ever offend you.
Hermione

Cruel one, why do you aggravate my miseries?
I fear to know myself in my present state.
Try not to believe all this you see; believe
I care no longer, boast that my victory   430
is perfect; believe my heart is iron against him;
alas, too, if you can, make me believe it.
You would have me run from him? Why, nothing prevents:
let us go, let us cease to envy his sorry conquest;
let his captive wholly rule him; let us fly. . . .   435
But if the thankless creature should find again
some place for duty, for honor, in his heart?
If he came begging mercy at my feet?
If to my terms, Love, you could bind him? If he
wished. . . . But the traitor wishes only my hurt.   440
And yet, let us remain, to trouble their fortune;
let us take some delight in molesting them—

or, forcing him to break such a solemn vow,
make him a criminal to all the Greeks.
I have brought down their hatred upon the son;   445
I would have them come again, to demand the mother.
Let us pay back these torments: let it be
that she must cause his ruin, or he her death.
Cleone
Do you think those eyes forever wide with tears
compete deliberately against your charms,   450
or that a heart so overwhelmed with misery
schemes to arouse the love of its persecutor?
Observe if she takes any comfort in it.
Why, then, is her soul lost in sadness? Why,
if he is welcome, so much proud disdain?   455
Hermione
Alas, to my sorrow, I listened and believed him.
I did not affect the mystery of silence:
I thought I could be sincere without danger; without
one guarded glance, one moment of resistance,
when I spoke to him, I trusted only my heart.   460
And who would not be candid as I was,
believing in a love so piously sworn?
Did he see me as he does today? You know,
you remember well, how all conspired for him:
my family avenged, the Greeks exultant,   465
our vessels laden with the plunder of Troy,
the exploits of his father topped by his own,
his love I believed more passionate than mine,
my heart—and you, too, dazzled by him: you all
betrayed me, before he did. But it's done, Cleone.   470
Whatever Pyrrhus may be, Hermione
can feel. There is virtue in Orestes. At least
he is able to love, even without being loved;
and perhaps, in time, he can accomplish that.
Let us go: let him come, then.   475
Cleone

                                   He arrives, madam.
Hermione
Ah, but I did not think he was so near!

(Enter Orestes.)

Shall I believe some trace of old affection
has brought you here to a sad princess, my lord,
or must I credit to your duty alone
the happy eagerness you have had to see me?   480
Orestes
Such is the fatal blindness of my love;
you know it, madam. Orestes' destiny
is to return unceasingly to adore you,
and to swear always he will not return.
I know what wounds your glance will open. I know   485
each step in your direction is self-betrayal;
I know it, I am ashamed. But by the Gods,
who saw the violence of my last goodbye,
I swear I have gone wherever sure extinction
would quit me of my vows and end my pain.   490
I have sought, I have begged, for death, among cruel tribes
who appease their gods with human blood alone.
They shut me from their temple; those barbarians,
before my willing blood, grew abstinent.
At last I have come to you, compelled to seek,   495
here in your eyes, elusive death. I have come
despairing, foreseeing only their indifference:
they need but take from me a shadow of hope;
now, to bring close the death I am bound to find,
they need but say what they have always said.   500
This, for a year, has been my one concern.
Madam, it is your part to take a victim
of whom a Scythian horde would have deprived you,
if I had met with any as cruel as you.
Hermione
Enough, my lord, enough of this mournful talk.   505
Greece charges you with a more pressing concern.
What's this of the Scythian and my cruelty?
Take thought for all those kings whom you represent.
Must their revenge now turn on a fit of passion?
In short, is it Orestes' blood they demand?   510
Discharge your appointed task.

Orestes
>   It was discharged
> well enough, madam, when Pyrrhus rejected it.
> He sends me back to Greece. Some other power
> disposes him to champion Hector's son.

Hermione
> The traitor!

Orestes
>   So that now, before I leave,   515
> I come to speak with you of my own fate.
> It seems to me already I hear the answer
> your hatred secretly intends for me.

Hermione
> What now? Unjust as ever, sad as ever,
> you still complain of my enmity? This harshness   520
> you have so many times alleged, what is it?
> I came to Epirus, where I had been consigned;
> my father willed it: but who knows, since then,
> whether I have not secretly shared your grief?
> Do you imagine you alone have been troubled?   525
> Do you think Epirus has not seen my tears?
> Who, I say, told you that, against my duty,
> I have not sometimes wished to see you?

Orestes
>   You wished
> to see me! Ah, divine princess . . . And still,
> I beg you, is it to me those words are said?   530
> Open your eyes: this is Orestes before you,
> Orestes, so long the object of their wrath.

Hermione
> Yes, it is you, who knew their youngest charms,
> who taught me, first, their power to wound; it is you,
> whom a thousand virtues forced me to admire,   535
> you whom I pitied, whom I wish to love.

Orestes
> I understand you. Such is my dismal lot:
> the heart for Pyrrhus, the wishes for Orestes.

Hermione

    Ah, do not envy the destiny of Pyrrhus.

    How I should hate you!   540

Orestes

                        You would love me more.

    In what a different light you would see me then!

    You wish to love me, and I cannot win you;

    but then, obedient to love's power alone,

    wishing to hate, you would be forced to love.

    O Gods! So much respect, such true affection: 545

    how all would speak for me, if you could hear me!

    You alone plead for Pyrrhus now—against

    your will, it may be, surely against his:

    for, have no doubt, he hates you; charmed by another,

    he can no longer—   550

Hermione

                Who told you, sir, he hates me?

    Have his looks, his words, informed you? Do you think

    the sight of me contemptible, that the love

    it wakens in a heart dies out so soon?

    Others see me, perhaps, more favorably.

Orestes

    Go on. How generous to hurl these insults!   555

    So, cruel one, it is I that scorn you here?

    Your eyes have found me wanting in constancy?

    I, then, am witness to their lack of power?

    I have scorned them? Ah, they would be well rejoiced

    to see my rival scorn them as I do.   560

Hermione

    What is his hatred or his love to me?

    Go, let all Greece be armed against a rebel;

    go, and, returning, bring the just reward

    of his rebellion. Let them make of Epirus

    a second Troy. Now will you say I love him?   565

Orestes

    Madam, do more, and come with me to Greece.

    Would you stay here to be a hostage? Come,

    return. Let your eyes speak to every heart.

    Let us make of our hatred a single force.

Hermione
But meanwhile, if he marries Andromache?   570
Orestes
So, madam!
Hermione
        Think of the disgrace for us,
that he should marry a Phrygian!
Orestes
               And you hate him?
Madam, accept it: love is not a fire
we can lock up within us. We are betrayed
by everything—our speech, our silence, our look;   575
and the ill-smothered flames start up more lively.
Hermione
Sir, it is clear, your stubborn soul breathes out
upon my words the venom from which it dies,
looks always for some subtlety, and thinks
hatred, in me, an acute stress of love.   580
I must explain myself, then you will act.
You know my duty brought me to this place;
my duty keeps me here; I cannot leave
unless my father or Pyrrhus orders it.
In my father's name, make Pyrrhus understand   585
no enemy of Greece can be my husband.
Make him decide between the Trojan and me.
Which one of us will he abandon? In short,
let him release me or give up the child.
Farewell. If he consents, I am ready to go.   590
           (Exeunt Hermione and Cleone.)
Orestes (alone)
Yes, yes, you will return with me, never fear;
I answer for him now. And, to be sure,
I have no fear that Pyrrhus will detain her:
he can see nothing but his precious Trojan;
all else annoys him; and today, perhaps,   595
he wants only a pretext to dismiss her.
We have only to confer: it is done. What joy
to take from Epirus such a splendid prey!
Keep all that's left of Troy and Hector, keep

his son, his widow, a thousand others still,   600
Epirus: it is enough that Hermione
should leave your shores forever, and your prince.
But by good luck he is coming. Let us speak.
Eros, to all that beauty close his eyes!

(Enter Pyrrhus and Phoenix.)

Pyrrhus

I was looking for you, sir. Some passing temper   605
made me resist the force of your arguments,
I must confess. Since I took leave of you
I have seen their justice, felt their cogency.
I have thought, like you, that toward Greece,
    toward my father—
in one word, toward myself—I was growing perverse.   610
I was enabling Troy to rise, impairing
all that Achilles did and that I have done.
I will condemn no more a righteous anger:
my lord, you will receive your victim.

Orestes

                         My lord,
by this severity and prudence, you buy   615
peace with the blood of an unfortunate.

Pyrrhus

Yes, but I would secure it even more:
Hermione is the gage of eternal peace.
I am marrying her. It seemed a pomp so lovely
awaited only your presence, to witness it.   620
You act for Greece and for her father: in you
Menelaus sees his brother live again.
Go, then, speak to her. Say I await tomorrow
from your hand, with the pledge of peace, her heart.

Orestes

O Gods!   625

(Exit Orestes.)

Pyrrhus

            Well, Phoenix, is love the master now?
You are still unsure? Your eyes refuse to know me?

Phoenix

I know you, sir: this good asperity

restores you to the Greeks and to yourself.
No more the plaything of a servile love,
this is Pyrrhus, Achilles' son and rival,   630
whom honor, in the end, recalls to its use,
who gains a second victory over Troy.

Pyrrhus

Say, rather, my first triumph begins today:
from this day only, I enjoy my fame.
My heart, as proud as you have seen it abject,   635
believes it has conquered a thousand enemies
in conquering love. Think, Phoenix, what I avoid,
what host of evils love draws in its train,
what friends, what duties I should have sacrificed,
what dangers—at a single glance forgotten!   640
All Greece would have united to crush a rebel.
For her, it seemed a pleasure to be destroyed.

Phoenix

Indeed I bless the happy cruelty
that gives you back—

Pyrrhus

        You saw how she treated me.
I thought, seeing her tenderness aroused,   645
her son would send her back to me disarmed:
I went to see the effect of his embraces;
I found nothing but tears and angry words.
Her grief embitters her, and, ever fiercer,
a hundred times she called on Hector. In vain   650
I swore to take her son's part. "This is Hector,"
she would say, embracing him: "See, here, his eyes,
his mouth, and see, already, his fearlessness;
it is he; it is you, dear husband, I embrace."
What is she thinking? Does she imagine, now,   655
I shall let her keep a son to nourish her love?

Phoenix

That, doubtless, would have been your thanks. But, sir,
forget her.

Pyrrhus

      I know what flatters her: her beauty
reassures her; the vain creature looks to see me,

despite my anger, at her knees again.   660
I should see her at my own, Phoenix, unmoved.
She is the widow of Hector, I am Pyrrhus,
Achilles' son; there is too much hate between us.
Phoenix
Begin, then, by not speaking to me of her.
Go to Hermione. Content to please her,   665
forget all, even your anger, at her feet.
Come, now, yourself: dispose her to this marriage.
Should it be trusted to a rival? He loves her
only too much.
Pyrrhus
            Do you think, if I marry her,
Andromache, in her heart, will not be jealous?   670
Phoenix
What! Still and only Andromache? By the Gods,
what is her joy or her despite to you?
What charm draws you to her, against your will?
Pyrrhus
No, I have not yet told her what she must hear:
she has seen but half my anger; she does not know   675
to what degree I am her enemy.
Let us return. I would show my scorn to her face,
and give my hatred a more liberal scope.
Come, Phoenix, see her proud charms mortified.
Let us go.   680
Phoenix
            Go, sir, and fling yourself at her feet;
go, and, protesting that your soul adores her,
encourage her to some new insolence.
Pyrrhus
I see. You think I am ready to excuse her,
to ease my heart.
Phoenix
            You love: that is enough.
Pyrrhus
Love her? One without gratitude, who hates me,   685
who, flattered by my love, hates me the more?
Kinless and friendless—hopeless, but for me.

26

I can condemn her son. Perhaps I should:
a foreigner, indeed a slave in Epirus,
I offer her her son, myself, my empire,   690
and I can win in her perfidious heart
no other rank than that of her persecutor?
No no, I have sworn it, my revenge is certain;
for once, her hatred shall be justified.
I am casting off her son. What tears will flow!   695
By what name will her sorrow call me now?
What spectacle is being prepared for her!
She will die, Phoenix, and I shall be the cause:
I myself plunge a dagger in her breast.

Phoenix

Then why declare you will do it? A moment past,   700
why did you not reflect how weak you are?

Pyrrhus

I hear you. But excuse some lingering fondness.
You fear my anger will give way so soon?
This is the last glow of a dying love.
Come, on with it. I obey your counsels, Phoenix.   705
Must I yield her son? Must I see Hermione?

Phoenix

Yes, my lord, see her, and with chastened vows
Protest to her—

Pyrrhus

       Let us do all I've promised.

ACT THREE

(*Enter Orestes and Pylades.*)

Pylades

My lord, subdue this overpowering anger:
I do not know you; you are no longer yourself.   710
Let me—

Orestes

        No, you admonish me too late,
Pylades, I am tired of reason. I have borne
my life, my punishment, too long. I know
I must carry her away from here, or perish;
it is decided, I mean to bring it off.   715
Yes, I will do it.

Pylades

            Then she must be abducted;
I agree. But consider, meantime, where you are.
How will you look to others, behaving so?
Dissemble: let this agitation be still.
Command your eyes to keep the secret. These guards,   720
this court, the air about you, all are servile
to Pyrrhus—most of all, to Hermione.
Conceal your anger, above all, from her.
O Gods! Why did you see her in this state?

Orestes

And why indeed? Was I master of myself?   725
I was carried away. I came, perhaps, to threaten
at the same time the heartless girl and her lover.

Pylades

What would that fury have accomplished?

Orestes

                      And who,
tell me, would not be maddened by the blow
I have just received? He is marrying, he says,   730

28

Hermione tomorrow; to honor me,
he would accept her from my hand. I swear,
sooner this hand in the barbarian's blood—
Pylades
You accuse him, sir, of this strange turn of fate.
Yet, driven by his own schemes, he is perhaps   735
as worthy of your pity as you of mine.
Orestes
Not so; I know him. My despair flatters him:
but for myself, but for my love, he scorned her;
her charms, till then, escaped him; the cruel soul
would take her now only to snatch her from me.   740
Gods! It was settled: Hermione was won,
was about to vanish from his sight; her heart,
confused between hurt pride and love, awaited
but one rebuff to give itself; her eyes
were opening, Pylades; she could hear Orestes,   745
could speak, could pity. It needed but a word.
Pylades
You think so?
Orestes
              What of that flaming anger against
a thankless heart—
Pylades
               Never was he more loved.
Do you think, if he had yielded her to you,
a prompt excuse would not have kept her here?   750
Will you believe me? Sick of her false enticements,
rather than take her with you, abandon her
now, once for all. Would you be charged with a fury
who will detest you—who, all your life, regretting
the lost hope of a marriage nearly achieved,   755
will wish—
Orestes
           That is my reason for taking her.
Here all would smile upon her; and I, for my part,
shall I take with me only a futile rage?
Shall I wander off again and try to forget her?
No, no, I would have her share my torments. Too long   760

I have grieved alone. I am tired of being pitied.
Now, in my turn, I mean the inhuman creature
to fear me: her cruel eyes, condemned to weep,
shall answer me with all the names I have called them.

Pylades

So this will be the outcome of your mission: 765
Orestes the abductor!

Orestes

Does it matter?
When our States, avenged, rejoice in my useful work,
will her cruel heart rejoice the less in my tears?
How am I served, to be admired by Greece,
if in Epirus I am the laughing-stock? 770
What would you have? But to hide nothing from you,
my innocence, at last, begins to oppress me.
I do not know what unjust, ageless power
leaves crime in peace and persecutes innocence.
Recalling any part of my life, I see 775
only misfortunes that condemn the Gods.
Then let us merit their wrath, let us earn their hatred.
Let crime's pleasure precede its pain. But you,
why, wrongly, do you bring upon yourself
a wrath destined for me? Too much, too long, 780
my friendship burdens you: avoid my misery,
turn from my guilt. Dear Pylades, believe me,
pity misguides you. Let those perils be mine
of which I intend to have the full reward.
Take to the Greeks this child whom Pyrrhus yields. 785
Go now.

Pylades

Sir, let us abduct Hermione.
A brave heart through all danger wins to the light.
Guided by love, what cannot friendship do?
Come, let us rouse the spirit of all your Greeks.
Our ships stand by, the wind invites us. I know 790
all the dark inner windings of this palace:
You see how the tide breaks upon its walls;
tonight, with ease, by a secret corridor
your quarry will be taken into your ship.

Orestes
   Dear friend, I abuse your friendship; yet be good   795
   to griefs that move your pity alone. Forgive
   a wretched man who loses all he loves,
   whom others hate, who hates himself. If only
   I, in my turn, may in a happier time—
Pylades
   My lord, dissemble; that is all I wish.   800
   Do not reveal your purpose before the act:
   meantime, forget Hermione's unkindness,
   forget your love. She is coming now.
Orestes
                                    Be off.
   Look to her capture. I will play my part.
              (*Exit Pylades. Enter Hermione and Cleone.*)
   Well, through my skill your conquest is rewon;   805
   I have seen Pyrrhus: your wedding is at hand.
Hermione
   I am told so; and your purpose in coming here,
   I am assured, is to prepare me for this.
Orestes
   Then you will not rebel against his wishes?
Hermione
   Who would have guessed that he was not unfaithful,   810
   that his love would be so tardily displayed,
   that he would return to me when I was leaving?
   I grant you, he may fear Greece and obey
   his interest rather than his heart. My eyes
   have had for you a power more absolute.   815
Orestes
   No, madam, he is in love. I doubt no longer.
   Cannot your eyes do all they wish? And you,
   surely, had no wish to displease him.
Hermione
                                    My lord,
   what can I do? My good faith has been promised:
   shall I take back what he does not hold from me?   820
   Love does not guide the fortunes of a princess:
   there is no glory, for us, but to obey.

Yet I was leaving. You have seen how far
I was careless of my duty for your sake.

Orestes

Ah, cruel, how well you knew. . . . But each of us,   825
madam, may choose to whom his soul is given.
Yours was your own. I hoped, but, when all's said,
you could dispose of it without robbing me.
I blame, therefore, not you but fortune. And now,
why weary you with an insistent plaint?   830
Such is your duty, I acknowledge—and mine,
to spare you so unhappy an interview.

(*Exit Orestes.*)

Hermione

Did you expect such temperate indignation,
Cleone?

Cleone

            The pain that holds its tongue is worse.
I pity him the more that he was author   835
of his own grief, striking the fatal blow.
Reflect how long your marriage has been planned:
he spoke, madam, and Pyrrhus gives the word.

Hermione

You imagine Pyrrhus is afraid? Of what?
Some tribes who, for ten years, fled before Hector—   840
who, terrified by Achilles' loss, retreated
a hundred times in their burning ships? Who now,
but for his son's support, would still be seen
demanding Helen of the unpunished Trojans?
No, he does not war upon himself: he wills   845
all that he does; if he marries me, he loves me.
But let Orestes blame his sorrows on me;
have we no conversation but his tears?
Pyrrhus returns to us! Ah, but dear Cleone,
can you conceive Hermione's happiness?   850
Do you know who Pyrrhus is? Have you told yourself
the number of his exploits? But who can count them?
Intrepid, followed about by victory, charming,
faithful, at last: his glory wants in nothing.
Why, think—   855

Cleone

    Be secret; your rival comes, in tears,
 no doubt to cast her sorrows at your feet.

Hermione

 Gods! Can I never yield to joy? Let us go:
 what could I say to her?

      (*Enter Andromache and Cephissa.*)

Andromache

      Where are you hurrying,
 madam? Is it not sweet enough to see
 the widow of Hector weeping, at your knees?   860
 I do not come to show you jealous grief,
 to envy you a heart that yields to your grace.
 By a cruel hand, alas, I saw pierced through
 the only heart I ever cared to move:
 my love was set alight, long since, by Hector;   865
 with him it has been sealed in the tomb. But still
 a son is left me. You will know, some day,
 what long journey our love goes, for a son;
 But not—at least I hope you will never know—
 what mortal fear his interest can inspire   870
 when he alone, of all that could comfort us,
 is left, and one would take him from our arms.
 Alas! When, wearied by ten years of misery,
 Troy in its anger rose against your mother,
 I won my Hector's promise in her behalf: 875
 you can make Pyrrhus yield as I made him.
 What threat is a small boy who outlives his doom?
 Let me go hide him in some lonely island;
 let them but trust his mother's fears: with me,
 my son will have no precept but to weep.   880

Hermione

 I realize your sorrows; but a stern duty,
 my father having spoken, bids me keep still.
 It is he that incites Pyrrhus. If one must now
 make Pyrrhus gentle, who is more skilled than you?
 Your eyes have long ruled in his soul. Persuade him 885
 to give the order, madam: I will subscribe.

      (*Exeunt Hermione and Cleone.*)

33

Andromache
With what contempt her cruel lips refuse!
Cephissa
I should believe her and see Pyrrhus. One look
would set at naught Hermione and the Greeks—
but he comes after you. 890

(*Enter Pyrrhus and Phoenix.*)

Pyrrhus (*to Phoenix*)
                    Where is the princess?
Did you not tell me she was here?
Phoenix

                        I thought so.
Andromache (*to Cephissa*)
Now you observe what power my eyes have!
Pyrrhus

                                Phoenix,

What is she saying?
Andromache (*to Cephissa*)
                    I am rejected by all.
Phoenix
Come, my lord, let us follow Hermione.
Cephissa (*to Andromache*)
Why are you waiting? Break this stubborn silence. 895
Andromache
He has promised them my son.
Cephissa

                            He has still to yield him.

Andromache
No, no, my tears are idle. His death is sworn.
Pyrrhus (*to Phoenix*)
Will she condescend, at least, to look at us?
What pride!
Andromache (*to Cephissa*)
                I only make his anger worse.
Let us go. 900
Pyrrhus (*to Phoenix*)
            Come, to give Hector's son to the Greeks.
Andromache
Ah, my lord, stay! What do you mean to do?

34

If you give the son, give them the mother! You swore,
even today, such earnest vows of friendship!
O Gods! Can I at least not move your pity?
Have you condemned me without hope of grace?   905

Pyrrhus

Phoenix will tell you, I have given my word.

Andromache

You who were braving, for me, so many perils!

Pyrrhus

I was blind then; my eyes have opened. His life
could have been spared if you had wished it so,
but you have not so much as requested it.   910
That is all done.

Andromache

         Ah, sir, you understood
those sighs that feared to know themselves repulsed.
Forgive the bright fame of an honored birth
this last small pride that fears to importune.
You know it well: Andromache, but for you,   915
would never have embraced the knees of a master.

Pyrrhus

Untrue: you hate me. In your deepest soul
you fear you will be indebted to my love.
Even this son, this son so dearly prized,
if I had saved him you would love him less.   920
Hate, contumely—all combines against me;
you hate me more than all the assembled Greeks.
Enjoy at leisure such a noble wrath.
Come, Phoenix.

Andromache (to Cephissa)

        Let us join my husband.

Cephissa

                    Madam—

Andromache (to Cephissa)

And what more would you have me say? Do you think   925
he does not know my sorrows, who caused them all?
      (to Pyrrhus)
My lord, behold to what state you have brought me.
I have seen my father dead, our city in flames;

35

I have seen the lives of my family cut short,
my husband, bleeding, dragged in the dust, his son   930
sentenced to live in bondage, alone with me.
But what is a son's power! I breathe. I serve.
Even more, I have at times consoled myself
that I was here, not elsewhere; that, fortunate
in his misfortunes, the son of many kings,   935
if he must be enslaved, should bow to your laws:
I thought his prison would become his refuge.
Once Priam, suppliant, had Achilles' respect.
His son I imagined nobler still. Forgive,
dear Hector, my credulity! I could not   940
suspect your enemy of a crime; I thought him,
at last, despite himself, magnanimous.
Ah, if he only were—enough to yield us
to the tomb I have had reared to you, and there,
letting his hatred and our miseries end,   945
to leave unseparated those loved remains!

Pyrrhus

Go, Phoenix. I will join you.

                                              (*Exit Phoenix.*)
                            Madam, stay.
That son for whom you weep can still be spared.
Yes, with regret I know it: causing your tears,
I only give you arms against me. I thought,   950
in coming here, I brought more hatred with me.
But at least, madam, turn your eyes to me: see
if mine are those of a relentless judge
or an enemy intent upon your mischief.
Would you force me to betray you? To what end?   955
In your son's name, let us be done with hate.
It is I, at last, that bid you spare him. Must I
implore your mercy? Must I beg for his life?
Must I embrace your knees to ask his pardon?
Now for the last time: save him, save yourself.   960
I know what vows I break for you, what hatreds
I am bringing down upon me. I send away
Hermione: I place upon her forehead,
in lieu of crown, an everlasting affront.

36

I lead you to the temple washed for her rites;   965
I wreathe you with the fillet made for her head.
But this is an offer, madam, that may no longer
be scorned; believe me, you must perish, or reign.
My heart, crushed by a year of ingratitude,
will bear no more uncertainty. Those fears,   970
those threats, those groans, are ended. I must die
if you are lost, but I must die if I wait.
Reflect: I will come presently to take you
to the temple where your son will be brought before me;
there you will see me, madam, meek or furious,   975
give you the crown, or give him before your eyes
in sacrifice.

                                 (*Exit Pyrrhus.*)

Cephissa

             I told you, in spite of Greece,
  You would be mistress of your fate.
Andromache

                      Alas,
  what are the consequences of your words!
  I had suffered all but this, to condemn my son.   980
Cephissa

  Madam, fidelity to your husband has lived
  its season: too much virtue could make you guilty.
  He himself would persuade you to be kind.
Andromache

  What! Give him Pyrrhus for successor?
Cephissa

                    Your son,
  whom the Greeks take from you by force, demands it.   985
  Would Hector's spirit, after all, be shamed?
  Do you suppose he scorns a victorious king
  who calls you back to your ancestral rank,
  who treads your infuriated conquerors down,
  one who disowns the memory of his father,   990
  belying Achilles' deeds, proving them vain?
Andromache

  If he forgets them, must I not recall them?
  Not think of Hector, deprived of obsequies,

dragged in dishonor round our walls? Forget
his father, stricken to the ground at my feet,   995
his blood drenching the altar he held embraced?
Think, think, Cephissa, of that cruel night
which fell eternally for a whole people;
see Pyrrhus, his eyes flashing in the glare
of our burning palaces, who trampled his way   1000
across my murdered brothers; see him enter,
well-smeared with blood, cheering the carnage on;
recall the victors' cries, recall the cries
of the dying, choked in fire, put to the sword;
And, crazed among those horrors, Andromache: 1005
that is how Pyrrhus came into my view;
those are the glories with which he crowned himself;
there, indeed, is the husband you offer. No,
I will not be his accomplice; let him take us,
at will, for his last victims. To yield to him   1010
with all that rage and sorrow in my heart!

Cephissa

Then we must go and witness your son's death:
it waits for you alone. . . . You are trembling, madam.

Andromache

Ah, what a memory you wake! Is it so,
Cephissa? I am to see him perish, too,   1015
that son, my only joy, the image of Hector,
that son he left me as the gage of his love!
Alas, I remember: the day his courage forced him
to seek Achilles—or rather death—he asked
to see his son, and took him in his arms.   1020
"Dear wife," he said, striving to calm my tears,
"I do not know the issue. Here is my son
in earnest of my faith: if he loses me,
let him discover me again in you.
If you hold dear the memory of our joy,   1025
prove to the son how well you loved the father."
And I can see a blood so precious spilled!
And, with him, let his total lineage die!
Barbarous king, must he share my crime? If I hate,
is he guilty of my hate? Has he cried out   1030

against the murder of all his friends and kind?
Has he complained of wrongs he does not feel?
And yet, my son, you die if I do not stay
the sword held cruelly above you. I can
turn it aside, and I present you to it?   1035
No, you will not die, I cannot suffer it.
Let us find Pyrrhus. But no, find him for me.
Go, dear Cephissa.

Cephissa
                        What would you have me say?

Andromache
Say, for my son, my love is strong enough. . . .
Do you believe, in his heart, he has sworn his death?   1040
Can love provoke his savagery so far?

Cephissa
My lady, he will soon come back, enraged.

Andromache
Then go, assure him. . . .

Cephissa
                        Of what? Of your consent?

Andromache
Alas, is it still mine to give? O ashes
of a husband! Trojans! Father! O my child,   1045
your life is costly to your mother! Come.

Cephissa
Where, madam? To what purpose?

Andromache
                                Let us go
upon his tomb, to ask my husband's counsel.

ACT FOUR

(*Enter Andromache and Cephissa.*)

Cephissa
> Ah, I do not doubt! It is your husband that works
> this miracle in you: it is Hector, madam.   1050
> It is his will that Troy should rise again
> with that blest son whom he directs you to save.
> Pyrrhus has sworn it. Only now you heard him;
> he waited only for a word. Believe
> in his exuberance: father, scepter, allies,   1055
> he places all at your feet, content with your love.
> He makes you sovereign of himself, his people.
> Is this the conqueror who deserved such hate?
> Already, in noble anger against the Greeks,
> he is as watchful for your son as you: 1060
> against their fury, he leaves him his own guard;
> not to endanger him, he risks himself.
> But now the temple rites await; you have promised.

Andromache
> Yes, I will go. But let us see my son.

Cephissa
> Madam, what urgency? Enough that his sight   1065
> should be forbidden you no longer. Soon
> you will go freely, to lavish care upon him,
> and your embraces will be counted no more.
> What joy, to rear a child whom one sees grow,
> no longer as a slave, reared for his master,   1070
> but as the proud revival of many kings!

Andromache
> Cephissa, let us see him for the last time.

Cephissa
> What are you saying? O Gods!

Andromache
> My dear Cephissa!

40

I have no secret from you: your loyalty,
in my misfortune, has been clearly shown;   1075
but, in my turn, I had thought you knew me better.
What? Did you think Andromache could wrong
a husband who believes, while she is living,
he lives again; that, waking the agonies
of all those dead, I would trouble their repose   1080
in seeking mine? Is this the love I have sworn?
But his son perished and must be defended.
Pyrrhus, in marrying me, takes up his cause.
That is enough, I accept his word. I know
what Pyrrhus is: violent but sincere,   1085
Cephissa, he will go beyond his promise.
I put my trust in the Greeks' anger as well:
their hatred wins a father for Hector's son.
Since I must sacrifice myself, I give
my life, all that remains of it, to Pyrrhus;   1090
when I receive his pledge upon the altars
I'll bind him to my son with deathless ties.
But, fatal to myself alone, my hand
will then at once cut short a life forsworn,
saving my virtue, rendering what I owe   1095
Pyrrhus, my son, my husband, and myself.
There is my innocent stratagem, devised
by love, commanded by my husband. Alone,
I shall join Hector and my ancestors.
Cephissa, it is for you to close my eyes.   1100
Cephissa
Ah, do not think I could live on—
Andromache
        No, no,
Cephissa, I forbid you to follow me.
I leave my only treasure in your care:
if you lived for me, live now for Hector's son.
As the sole guardian of the Trojans' hope,   1105
think of those many kings who look to you.
Stay close to Pyrrhus; help him keep his word:
if there is need, you may speak to him of me.
Show him the gravity of this marriage; recall

that I was sworn to him before my death;   1110
say that his bitterness should be composed,
that leaving him my son is a high tribute.
Let my son know the heroes of his race;
as much as possible, guide him in their steps:
tell him their exploits, rather what they did   1115
than what they were; speak to him, day by day,
of his father's virtues, and speak sometimes, too,
of his mother. But, Cephissa, let him not dream
of avenging us. We leave him with a master
whom he must reconcile and strive to please.   1120
Guard him from being vain of his ancestry:
he is of Hector's blood, but the last of it;
and for this remnant I have sacrificed,
in a single day, my life, my hatred, my love.

Cephissa

Alas!   1125

Andromache

      Do not come with me if you know
you have not the courage to restrain your grief.
Someone approaches. Hide your tears. Remember,
the fate of Andromache is in your hands.
It is Hermione. Let us fly from her rage.

                (*Exeunt Andromache and Cephissa.*
                       Enter Hermione and Cleone.)

Cleone

No, I shall not be done with marveling   1130
that you keep silence, madam. This cruel contempt
has not, even slightly, put your spirits about?
You peacefully endure such a rude attack,
you who would shudder at the very name
of Andromache, who were thrown into despair   1135
if Pyrrhus sought to honor her with a glance?
He is marrying her, and with his diadem
he gives the promise lately sworn to you.
And still your lips, mute to such provocation,
disdain to yield him one reproachful word?   1140
Ah, but I fear so sinister a calm!
It would be better—

Hermione
Have you sent for Orestes?

Cleone
He is coming, madam, he is coming. You know
he would soon be stationed at your feet, prepared
to serve forever with no hope of reward: 1145
your eyes are all too sure of enchanting him.
He is here.

(*Enter Orestes.*)

Orestes
Ah, madam! Is it true for once
that, in coming here, Orestes does your will?
Have I been flattered by an idle hope?
Did you really want me? Shall I believe your eyes,   1150
putting their armor off, see me at last
and wish—

Hermione
I wish to know, sir, if you love me.

Orestes
Love you? O Gods! My vows, my forsworn vows,
my flight and my return, my homage, my curses,
my hopelessness, my tear-drowned eyes: what proofs   1155
will you believe if you do not believe them?

Hermione
Avenge me, and I do.

Orestes
Then, madam, come,
to set once more the flame of anger to Greece;
writing my courage and your name in fire,
you will take Helen's place, I Agamemnon's;   1160
let us revive Troy's misery in this land,
and, like our fathers, be on the tongues of men.
Let us sail now. I am ready.

Hermione
No, let us stay:
I will not bear such injuries so far.
What! Shall I crown that insolence with pride,   1165
going far off, to wait for a slow vengeance?
Shall I rely upon the fortunes of war,

43

which in the end might fail me? When I go,
I mean that all Epirus shall be in tears.
But if you avenge me, do it within an hour.   1170
For me, all your postponements are refusals.
To the temple, quickly: you must destroy—

Orestes

Whom?

Hermione

Pyrrhus.

Orestes

Pyrrhus, madam?

Hermione

So, then, your hatred weakens?
Go. Run! And fear that I may call you back.
Do not allege the rights I wish to forget;   1175
it is not for you to justify him.

Orestes

I?

I would excuse him? Madam, your own goodness
has marked his guilt too deeply upon my soul.
Let us have vengeance, yes, but in other ways:
as his enemies, but not as his assassins.   1180
Let his ruin be a lawful conquest. Shall I,
for answer to the Greeks, come bearing his head?
Have I taken upon myself the nation's cause
only to seal my diligence with murder?
In the Gods' name, let Greece make known her will,   1185
and let him die convicted by public hate.
Do not forget: he reigns, and a crowned head—

Hermione

Is it not enough for you that I condemn him?
Is it not enough that my offended name
demands a victim for myself alone;   1190
that Hermione is the prize of a tyrant's death;
that I hate him; and, to say all, that I loved him?
I do not hide it: the sullen wretch could charm me,
whether my love or my father ordained it so,
no matter; but, in short, be guided by that.   1195

For all his shameful mockery of my vows,
for all my righteous horror of his crime,
while he is living, fear that I may forgive him.
Doubt my uncertain anger: I may well
love him tomorrow, unless he dies today.   1200

Orestes

Why, then, he must be lost, beyond reprieve;
he must. . . . And yet what is it that I must do?
How can I serve your enmity so soon?
By what path will my anger seek him out?
I have scarcely reached Epirus, and at once   1205
you would overturn an empire with my hands,
destroy a king; and for his punishment
you give me but a day, an hour, a moment;
I must strike him down before his people's eyes!
Let me conduct my victim to the altar;   1210
I object no more; I would only look about me
and know the place where I must immolate him:
tonight I serve you, tonight I attack.

Hermione

                        But meanwhile
he is marrying Andromache today;
the throne already stands in the temple, my shame   1215
is manifest, his crime is perfect. In short,
why are you waiting? He offers you his life:
he is going without precautions, without guards,
to this festival; he has placed them round Hector's son;
he walks exposed to whatever hand will serve me.   1220
Would you protect his life against his will?
Arm all my followers, let them join your Greeks;
quickly stir up your friends; all mine are yours.
I am betrayed. You are mocked. We are all despised.
Even now their hatred equals mine: it spares   1225
unwillingly the bridegroom of a Trojan.
Speak out: my enemy shall not escape you,
or rather, you have only to let them strike.
Whether you lead or follow that splendid fury,
come back to me all dressed in the traitor's blood;   1230
go: in that state, be certain of my heart.

45

Orestes
  But, madam, think—
Hermione
                    Ah, sir, this is too much!
  So many arguments insult my anger.
  I wished to offer you the key to my love,
  to make Orestes happy; but he would still   1235
  complain and deserve nothing. Go away:
  go, boast to others of your constancy,
  and leave me here to work my vengeance out.
  My weak kindnesses put my heart to shame;
  this is one more refusal than enough   1240
  in a single day. I will go from here, alone,
  to the temple, where you dare not go to win me.
  There I will find the way to my enemy;
  I will pierce through the heart I could not touch.
  And my bloody hands, turning upon myself,   1245
  in spite of him, will join our destinies;
  and cruel as he is, I shall find it sweeter
  to die with him than to live with you.
Orestes
                              No, madam,
  I shall deprive you of that mortal pleasure:
  Orestes' hand, no other, will strike him down.   1250
  The task of putting your enemies to death
  is mine, and you may thank me as you will.
Hermione
  Go. Leave the guidance of your fate to me,
  and let your ships be ready for our flight.

                                    (*Exit Orestes.*)

Cleone
  You will be ruined, madam; and you should think—   1255
Hermione
  Ruined or not, I think of my revenge.
  I am still not sure, whatever he may have sworn,
  that I should trust it to another: Pyrrhus
  is not so guilty in Orestes' eyes
  as in my own. My blows would be struck more surely.   1260
  What joy to take my own revenge, to draw

my arm away bright with the perjurer's blood,
and, for his keener pain, my keener pleasure,
to obscure my rival from his dying gaze!
Ah, if at least Orestes, striking, leaves him   1265
the bitter certainty that he dies my victim!
Go, find him: tell him the churl must understand
he is sacrificed to my hatred, not to Greece.
Run, dear Cleone: my revenge is lost
unless he knows, in dying, it is I that kill him.   1270

Cleone

I will obey you. But what is this? O Gods!
Who would have thought it likely, madam? The King.

Hermione

Ah, my Cleone, follow Orestes: tell him
he must do nothing till he sees me again!

(*Exit Cephissa. Enter Pyrrhus and Phoenix.*)

Pyrrhus

I was not expected, madam, and it is clear   1275
my presence here disturbs your interview.
I do not come, armed with unworthy craft,
to give my injustice a show of equity;
enough that my heart condemns me; I should argue
with little force what I do not believe.   1280
I am marrying a Trojan. Yes, it is true,
I gave you the same pledge I am giving her.
Another would recall to you that our fathers,
in the Trojan fields, without us, forged those bonds;
that then, without consulting your choice or mine,   1285
we were bound lovelessly; but, for myself,
it is enough that I submitted. My heart
was promised to you by my ambassadors.
Far from opposing them, I wished to assent:
I saw you arrive with them in Epirus; and though,   1290
even then, the conquering flame of other eyes
had come between me and the power of yours,
I would not be deterred by that new longing:
I obstinately wished to be true to you;
I welcomed you as a queen; and to this day   1295
I have thought my promises would serve for love.

47

But it is love that wins. By a fatal stroke,
Andromache takes from me a heart she detests:
forced on, one by the other, we go to the altar
to swear, despite ourselves, an immortal love.   1300
Knowing this, madam, cry out against a traitor
who is one with sorrow, yet who wills to be.
Far from repressing that well-founded rage,
I shall be eased, perhaps, as much as you.
Give me whatever names are due to perjurers: 1305
I fear your silence, not your abuse; my heart,
calling a thousand secret witnesses,
the less you speak, will have the more to say.
Hermione
Sir, this confession stripped of artifice
at least, I am glad to see, renders you justice.   1310
It is well that, breaking such a solemn vow,
you yield yourself to crime like a criminal.
Is it fitting, after all, that a conqueror stoop
to the servile law of keeping promises?
No, no, it is rather perfidy that tempts you,   1315
and you have sought me only to boast of it.
What? Held by neither oath nor duty, to court
a Greek, loving a Trojan? To cast me off,
to take me back, to return from Helen's daughter
once more to Hector's widow? To crown, by turns,   1320
the captive and the princess; to sacrifice
Troy to the Greeks and Greece to Hector's son?
All this belongs to a heart that rules itself,
to a hero unenslaved by his solemn word.
To please your bride, I should be lavish, perhaps,   1325
with the fine names of perjurer and traitor.
You come to observe my pallor, that you may go
and mock my grief, in her arms. You would have me seen,
weeping, behind her chariot; but, my lord,
that would be too much joy in a single day.   1330
Rather than look about you for new titles,
will you not be content with those you bear?
The valor, flung to earth, of the old father
of Hector, dying before his family's eyes,

while your arm, driven into his breast, seeks out   1335
a last poor drop of blood frozen with age;
Troy alight, falling into rivers of blood;
while all your Greeks in indignation watch,
your hand slashing Polyxena's throat: what glory
can one refuse to these great-hearted deeds?   1340

Pyrrhus

Madam, I know to what excess of rage
the task of avenging Helen carried me;
I may well deplore, to you, the blood I shed;
but that is past. I thank heaven your contempt
shows me how blameless my happy longing is.   1345
My heart, it seems, has been too quickly troubled;
it should have known you better, searched itself
more deeply. My scruples did you a mortal wrong.
I see it well: we must believe ourselves
loved, to believe ourselves unfaithful. But you   1350
had no such claim to hold me in your power.
I fear to disappoint you; perhaps I serve you.
Our hearts have had no mutual need. I wished
to obey my duty, you submitted to yours:
nothing, in fact, required that you should love me.   1355

Hermione

I have not loved you? What, then, have I done?
I have scorned, for you, the pleading of all our princes;
I have sought you out in the depth of your provinces;
here I still am, despite your betrayals, despite
the anger of all my Greeks, shamed by my goodness.   1360
I have ordered them to hide my indignity;
I waited, in secret, a perjurer's return;
soon or late, I believed, recalled to your duty,
you would bring back the heart that was my right.
I cherished you inconstant; what would I have done,   1365
faithful? Now, even now, when your cruel mouth
so calmly speaks my death sentence, I wonder,
cold wretch, I wonder still, if I do not love you.
But, sir, if it must be, if heaven in anger
intends another to glory in your desire,   1370
be done, be married: so be it; but at least

do not compel my eyes to witness it.
I speak to you for the last time perhaps.
Wait but one day. Tomorrow you will triumph. . . .
You do not answer? Treacherous one, I see it,   1375
you count each moment you are losing with me.
Your heart, impatient to rejoin your Trojan,
is galled that another should address you. You speak
to her in silence; your eyes, wandering, search
for her. I will not detain you. Be gone from here.   1380
Go, make the eternal vow I have heard you make;
swear impiously before the sovereign Gods,
those just Gods who by no means have forgotten
that we were bound by the same promise. Away:
to the altar with a heart that rejects me. Go,   1385
run; but fear, still, to find Hermione there.

                                                        (*Exit.*)

Phoenix

My lord, you hear: beware a furious woman
who loves and seeks revenge. She is all too well
supported here; her quarrel is bound up
with the Greek cause; Orestes loves her still.   1390
Perhaps at such a price—

Pyrrhus

                    Andromache
is waiting for me. Phoenix, guard her son.

ACT FIVE

Hermione (alone)

Where am I? What have I done? What must I do?
What frenzy overtakes me? What grief devours me?
Wandering, aimless, I circle through this palace. 1395
Ah! Can I not know if I love or hate?
His cruel eyes! With what look they dismissed me:
unpitying, without even affected pain!
Did I see him troubled or sorry for a moment?
Could I draw from him one kindly murmur? He stood 1400
mute to my sighs, untouched by my dismay,
my tears. Did he even seem to have part in them?
And I am anxious! To crown my wretchedness,
my heart, my coward heart, is concerned for him!
I quake to think he is threatened! At the point 1405
of eager vengeance, I already forgive!
No. Let our judgment not be stayed: let him die.
For, certainly, he lives no longer for us.
The recreant triumphs, mocks my rage, believes
this storm will dissipate itself in tears, 1410
that, weak as ever, brave by fits and starts,
I'll fend off with one arm the blows of the other.
He is judging me by my past goodness. But he,
more likely, has quite different thoughts: he triumphs
in the temple now, and does not seek to know 1415
if others, elsewhere, wish him life or death.
He leaves me in this fatal uncertainty.
No, no I say again, let Orestes act.
Death: since he must indeed have known the hazard,
and since indeed he forces me to wish it. 1420
To wish it? What? It is I, then, that ordain it?
His death will be the work of Hermione's love?
That prince, whose brilliant deeds my heart retold
in former days with such delight, to whom

even in secret I had destined myself   1425
before this fatal match was sworn—so, then,
I have crossed these many seas and states, I have come
so far, only to plot his death, to attack,
to destroy him? Ah, before he dies—

                                        (*Enter Cleone.*)
                        Cleone,
what have I done? What do you come to tell me?   1430
What is Pyrrhus doing?
Cleone

                        He is upon the crest,
proudest of mortals and the most in love.
I saw him, like a returning conqueror, lead
his new prize toward the temple, drinking in,
through eyes brilliant with joy and expectation,   1435
the intoxicating pleasure of her sight.
Andromache, through a thousand joyful cries,
takes to the altars her memory of Troy;
incapable of loving and hating still,
she seems to obey, not glad but not repining.   1440
Hermione

And he? He has carried off the outrage? Cleone
did you observe him well? Did it seem to you
his happiness was perfect and unafraid?
Did he not turn his eyes back toward the palace?
Tell me, did you not show yourself to him?   1445
Did the scoundrel blush to see you? Did his face,
his troubled look, expose his lying heart?
Did he bear himself so proudly to the end?
Cleone

My lady, he sees nothing: his safety, his glory—
all seems to have taken flight, with you, from his mind.   1450
Careless of who may follow him, enemies
or subjects, he presses to his amorous goal.
He has placed his guard round Hector's son, believing
no other life is threatened. Phoenix himself
is charged with it: he has put the child in a fort   1455
well distant from the temple and the palace.
This, in his joy, is the King's one concern.

Hermione
False heart! He'll die. What did Orestes say?
Cleone
Orestes, with his Greeks, went into the temple.
Hermione
Well, then? Is he not bent upon serving me?   1460
Cleone
I do not know.
Hermione
    You do not know? What now?
Orestes, too, betrays me?
Cleone
     He worships you;
but, baited by a thousand qualms, he listens
now to his love, now to his honor. In Pyrrhus
he respects the dignity of the crown. He respects   1465
Achilles. He respects Pyrrhus himself.
He fears the Greeks, the world's reproof—but fears
himself, he says, even more. He would come back
like a hero, bringing you the enemy's head,
but to be called assassin dismays, deters him.   1470
In short, he entered, not knowing if he would leave
as a culprit or a bystander.
Hermione
     No, no,
he will see them triumph without an obstacle;
he will be wary of troubling this great event.
I know from what misgivings his courage suffers: 1475
the coward fears death, and that is all he fears.
Why, without asking it, my mother armed
all Greece in tribute to herself; she saw,
during ten years of combat, twenty kings,
whom she did not even know, die in her cause.   1480
And I? I ask but a perjurer's death. I entrust
my grievance to a lover, who at this price
can take me, without risk; I give myself,
and cannot be avenged! Come, let us go.
It is for me alone to have justice. Let screams   1485
of anguish sound in the temple; let us cut short

53

the last of their fatal wedding; so, with luck,
they will be joined but for a moment. I'll strike
blindly in that wild uproar: all, for me,
will be Pyrrhus, even Orestes. I shall die,   1490
but not, at least, without requital in death,
and not alone. Some other will go with me.

> (*Enter Orestes.*)

Orestes

Madam, it is all done: you are satisfied.
Pyrrhus yields at the altar his faithless life.

Hermione

He is dead?   1495

Orestes

        He is dying, and our angry Greeks
have washed away his treacheries in his blood.
I promised it to you; and though my heart
foresaw but ruin in that conspiracy,
I ran to the temple, where our Greeks, dispersed,
slipped through the crowd up to the altar. Pyrrhus   1500
saw me, but gave no sign. Rather it seemed
the glimpse of me excited his recklessness,
as though, defied in her ambassador,
all Greece heightened the splendor of his nuptials.
At last, with fierce joy, taking his diadem,   1505
he himself placed it on Andromache's brow.
He said: "I give my crown and promise. Reign,
Andromache, over Epirus, over me.
I pledge your son a father's steadfast love;
I call the Gods to witness, I swear to you,   1510
his mother, that all his enemies are mine;
I recognize him as the king of the Trojans."
To these words, which were drawing the crowd's assent,
our Greeks responded but with a cry of rage.
The traitor saw himself closed round; my arm   1515
could find no room to strike: one with another
vied in the glory of the kill. I watched him
lashing about among their hands awhile,
wounds streaming, as he tried to avoid their blows;
but, stumbling to the altar, at last he fell.   1520

I made my way through the terror-stricken crowd,
that I might quickly take my princess from here
and reach the port, where soon our friends will come,
their bodies dyed with the blood I promised you.

Hermione

What have they done?   1525

Orestes

                Forgive them their impatience:
they were, I know, unmindful of your revenge;
you wished my hand to be the first to strike,
that, dying, he should be certain he died for you;
but it was I whose ardor set them on:
for you alone I brought them into the temple;   1530
and you may justly claim as your own act
a death of which their arms were but instruments.
You alone struck—

Hermione

             Be still, traitor. Impute
your cowardly parricide* but to yourself.
Go, let your Greeks applaud your madness. Go: 1535
I disown it. You are horrible to me.
What have you done, barbarian? With what fury
have you cut off so admirable a life!
Savages, could you butcher him today,
and all your blood not rise to take his part?   1540
Speak: who has made you arbiter of his fate?
Why murder him? For what crime? By what right?
Who told you so?

Orestes

           O Gods! What? Did you not
yourself, here, even today, order his death?

Hermione

Should one believe a woman crazed with love?   1545
Should you not still have read my deepest thought?
Did you not see, in all my helpless rages,
my heart belied my mouth? And if I had wished it,
must you have given assent? Should you not still

---

* Racine uses the word in its most general sense: the murder of any person whom one is
bound in honor to respect.

have forced me to repeat it a hundred times,   1550
and, before acting, returned to know my counsel,
and returned again—or rather, avoided me?
Could you not leave me to revenge myself?
What brings you to this country where I have fled
to escape you? See the detestable fruit of your love: 1555
you brought me the misfortune that follows you.
It is you whose mission, deadly to us both,
urged him, to his undoing, toward my rival.
We should still see him sharing his kindnesses;
perhaps he would love me; he would pretend, at least.   1560
Goodbye. Go, as you will. I remain in Epirus.
I renounce Greece and Sparta, its sovereign power,
and all my family; enough, traitor, for me
that it should bear a monster such as you.

(Exeunt Hermione and Cleone.)

Orestes (alone)
Who is this? Hermione? What have I heard?   1565
For whom does the blood flow I have lately shed?
To believe her, I am a traitor, an assassin.
Can it be Pyrrhus that dies? Am I Orestes?
I stifle in my heart the reason that lights me;
I put to death, with sorrow, a king I revere;   1570
I violate, in a day, the rights of sovereigns,
those of ambassadors, all those of mankind,
even the sanctity of altars—become
a parricide, a cutthroat, a desecrator.
For whom? For a heartless woman I swear to serve,   1575
who, unless he dies, will never see me again,
whose fury I espouse. And when I have done,
she asks me to give back his blood, his life;
she loves him! I am now a ravening monster!
She flies from me: her image fades from view,   1580
is gone forever, leaving for recompense
all the vile names I took to give her joy!

(Enter Pylades and soldiers.)

Pylades
We must be gone, sir. Let us leave this palace,
or else decide we shall never leave. For a moment

our Greeks defend its gate. The assembled people   1585
have taken arms, are coming to hunt us down.
All, here, obey Andromache: they accept her
as queen, consider us their enemies.
Andromache herself, so defiant of Pyrrhus,
now pays him all the homage of a good widow,   1590
commanding his revenge. Perhaps she would still
avenge, upon us, Troy and her first husband.
Let us not wait to be surrounded. Come,
our Greeks will join us; and while Hermione
still holds the people thronged about her, see,   1595
this way our path lies: let us go in safety.

Orestes

No, no, friends, it is Hermione I would follow:
I cannot live beyond her parting judgment.
Go: I have wrought the crime. I will expiate it.

Pylades

Hermione, sir? We must forget her. What?   1600
Still instrument and object of her anger,
you look for some new outrage among the dead?
Because she dies, must you die, too?

Orestes

                      She dies?

Gods! What is this?

Pylades

                So, then, you did not know?
Returning here, we met her as she was running,   1605
distraught and haggard, toward the temple. She saw
the body of Pyrrhus carried by some soldiers
who, excited by his blood, were crying revenge.
It was this, no doubt, that brought her violence on.
Presently, as we watched above the gate,   1610
we saw her, dagger in hand, lean over Pyrrhus,
then look at heaven, then stab herself, and fall.

Orestes

By the Gods' grace, my doom exceeds my hope.
Yes, heaven, I praise your steadfastness. Applied
unrestingly to my punishment, you have brought me   1615
to sorrow's zenith. Your hatred has found ease

shaping my misery: I had been born to serve
as an example of what your wrath can do,
to be a very nonesuch of misfortune.
Well, then, I die content, fulfilled. Where now 1620
are those two lovers? To complete my joy,
I must mix their blood with mine, be drowned in it;
I would look, dying, upon them both. Come, then,
we'll join three hearts that could not be reconciled.
But what thick night surrounds me all at once? 1625
Which way to turn? What makes me tremble? What horror
gripes me? Now, heaven be thanked, I begin to see. . . .
Gods! But what streams of blood are flowing round me!
Pylades
Ah, my lord!
Orestes
                What? Is it you, Pyrrhus, again?
Shall I meet everywhere a rival I loathe? 1630
Pierced with so many wounds, how have you fled?
Here, take the thrust I saved for you! What now?
Hermione, in my sight, embraces him?
She comes to snatch him from the threatening blow.
Gods! What a dreadful look she turns upon me! 1635
What fiends come in her train? What serpents slide?
Ho! Daughters of hell, are your hands ready? For whom
do you bring those serpents hissing upon your heads?
For whom the array that follows? Do you come
to carry me into the eternal night? 1640
Come. I surrender to your fierce desires.
But no, turn back, leave all to Hermione:
better than you, she'll tear me flesh from bone,
and in the end I bring her my heart to eat.
Pylades
He falls unconscious. Friends, the time runs out; 1645
let us use well what this wild access leaves us
to rescue him. Our efforts would be lost
if, with his senses, he recovered his rage.

BRITANNICUS

Voltaire called it the play of connoisseurs. Here, he said, Racine does not employ "seductions of erotic portraiture" but exposes his characters "with a perhaps altogether matchless penetration of psychological analysis."

It is true that some of the more perceptive among the court and the critics were the first to appreciate the restrained mood of his play, its understatement of notorious horrors. The public came over very soon, however, and the popularity of *Britannicus* has been as durable as that of political intrigue and private wickedness. Its portrait of the young Nero, at the moment when he begins to show clearly, and to enjoy, his sadistic tendencies, is as original as anything on the stage. Racine conceived him as "a budding monster": the fascination of the play is all in this verb.

But while the young emperor moves warily toward atrocity, it is the dominant presence of Agrippina, with her troubled memories and premonitions, that gives the play size and depth. Racine said that he stretched the life of Britannicus to make him seventeen: by this chronology Nero is twenty-two and Agrippina forty-four. It is the year of her death. To this beautiful, scheming woman, who has been virtually running the empire and means to continue, her son Nero and her stepson Britannicus are mere instruments of power. But the first rebels, and the second is lost to her through his very compliance. In *Andromaque* the ideal tragic attributes seemed to be shared among four characters; here, as Racine in effect pointed out, the tragic figure is twofold, consisting of Agrippina and Britannicus. Junia is a victim, through no fault or negligence of her own. The splendid Cornelian figure of Burrus could support a tragedy by itself: one can imagine the story rewritten, leaving his part almost intact, to give him the central place. But here he is not a protagonist. He represents all the good influences on Nero, opposing that of Narcissus; and the prominence given to him serves to bring out the inevitable as well as the perverse nature of the crime.

Racine attenuates Agrippina's historical reputation, letting us suppose that the evil rumors may have been calumnies brought on by her overbearing pride and maternal ambition. As the humiliated autocrat and offended mother, she commands a certain sympathy. In the last act, where she becomes embarrassing, almost ridiculous, in her premature triumph, she is most human; yet in this scene there is for the first time an inkling of the incestuous emotion at which Tacitus delights to hint. Tacitus is unsparing in his treatment of Agrippina the younger; he combines the known facts with a great deal of hearsay and conjecture, all of it equally convincing to him. But he does not attempt to conceal his admiration for her strategic genius and her tireless audacity. Nor does Racine: his portrait remains respectfully consistent with her image of herself as, at least, a semidivine being, one to whom "the self-seeking prayers of mortals" may be addressed. In both writers, each new aspersion is like a puff of incense.

This is most striking in the great "confession," her candid and fearless speech of self-defense in Act IV, which gives us a decade of Roman history (condensing books XII and XIII of the *Annals*) in a style as stringently documentary as its original, much of it literally translated from Tacitus. Racine wrote only one other speech as long—in *Mithridate*—but none that wastes fewer words. Here and elsewhere in the play he conveys, along with Tacitus' mordancy, his deeper and sternly compassionate meaning: the sense of a whole era helplessly pervaded by evil, of which his characters are as much the victims as the instruments. Erich Auerbach has defined it: "From the end of the first century of the Imperial Age something sultry and oppressive appears, a darkening of the atmosphere of life. It is unmistakable in Seneca [and in] the somber tone of Tacitus' historical writing." He adds that "Tacitus' figures (despite the contemporary tendency towards a merely sensory, graphic and gestural treatment) retain a great deal of intrinsic humanity and dignity."

It is by allowing his characters their due share of these qualities that

Racine sustains his tragic view of a demoralized world. In this, as in its psychological realism, the play is true to its great source. Yet we need to know nothing of its background to enjoy the play: there has been no more perfect dramatization of a narrative work.

Britannicus opened at the Bourgogne on December 13, 1669, a year to the day after the funeral of Mademoiselle du Parc, the young widowed actress whom Racine loved and for whom he had written the part of Andromache. The première was like another funeral. As Mary Duclaux tells it in her biography: "The shopkeepers of the rue Saint-Denis, who did not mind what they paid for their seats if they could be present on a First Night at the court theatre, were, for once in a way, attracted elsewhere by a still more dramatic representation: on the Place de Grève, a certain Huguenot marquis was to have his head cut off for high treason." The Bourgogne was more than half empty, and "amid the void of the boxes Corneille was to be seen conspicuous, gloating over his rival's discomfiture."

This was Racine's fifth play. He had followed *Andromaque* with another success, *Les Plaideurs,* his only comedy, satirizing the mania for litigation, a very free imitation of Aristophanes' *Wasps.* It was a wonderfully light-hearted piece written in the last year of his love affair, and it is still a favorite. Between *Britannicus* and *Phèdre* he had four great successes. Another Roman play, *Bérénice,* was compared to its advantage with one written simultaneously by Corneille on the same subject. Then Paris flocked to *Bajazet,* a tragedy of love and politics in a Turkish seraglio, and to *Mithridate,* Racine's most popular play in his own time. *Iphigénie,* in 1674, was praised from the beginning for its perfection of style and structure: some critics, particularly in the eighteenth century, have called it his masterpiece.

CHARACTERS

Nero
Emperor, son of Agrippina

Britannicus
Son of the emperor Claudius and of Messalina

Agrippina
Widow of Domitius Ahenobarbus, father of Nero; by a second marriage, widow of the emperor Claudius

Junia
Loved by Britannicus

Burrus
Tutor of Nero

Narcissus
Tutor of Britannicus

Albina
Confidante of Agrippina

Guards

The scene is at Rome, in a room of Nero's palace

ACT ONE

(Enter Agrippina and Albina.)

Albina

   So it has come to this, that while Nero sleeps
   you must wait here for him? That now, abroad
   in the palace without retinue, without guards,
   the mother of Caesar watches alone at his door?
   Madam, return to your apartments.   5

Agrippina

                                        Albina,
   I dare not be away, not even a moment.
   I will wait to see him. The sorrows he causes me
   are enough to occupy me while he sleeps.
   All I foretold is but too well assured.
   Nero has moved against Britannicus.   10
   The impatient Nero is done with self-restraint;
   he is weary of inspiring love: he would now
   be feared. Britannicus tortures him. I, in turn,
   feel my own presence daily more troublesome.

Albina

   You to whom Nero owes the life he breathes,   15
   who called him, from so far, to the emperorship—
   who, disinheriting the son of Claudius,
   made him, the fortunate Domitius, Caesar?
   All speaks to him in Agrippina's behalf:
   he owes you his love, madam.   20

Agrippina

                          He does, Albina.
   If he is noble-minded, all speaks for me,
   but if he is ungrateful, all against me.

Albina

   Ungrateful, madam? Why, all his conduct proves
   duty to be instilled into his soul.

63

For three full years, what has he said or done   25
that does not promise Rome a perfect emperor?
Rome thinks itself returned, under his reign,
to the era of its consuls: he governs it
like a father. Indeed, Nero in his youth
has the virtues of Augustus ripe with age.   30

Agrippina

No, no, my interest does not make me unjust:
he commences, it is true, where Augustus finished;
but fear that, as the future destroys the past,
he'll tend to finish as Augustus began.
He wears a vain disguise. I read in his face   35
the sad, wild humor of the Domitius blood.
He mixes with its self-infatuation
the stern pride of the Neros he took from me.
Tyranny always has a bright beginning:
Caligula, for a time, was the joy of Rome,   40
but, his affected goodness turning to madness,
Rome's joy became its horror. What, after all,
does it mean to me that Nero, more dutiful,
should leave, one day, the example of long virtue?
Have I put the tiller of the State in his hand   45
that he should steer by the people's, the senate's, whim?
Would he be the father of the fatherland?
Let him; but let him be somewhat more aware
that Agrippina is his mother.—What name,
however, to give the crime revealed this morning?   50
He knows well, for their love can be no secret,
that Junia is adored by Britannicus,
and this same Nero, whom virtue guides, procures
Junia's abduction in the dead of night.
What does he mean? Is it hatred that inspires him?   55
Is it love? Is it merely the pleasure of hurting them?
Or is it not that his malignity
punishes them because I have been their support?

Albina

You—their support, madam?

Agrippina

               Stop, dear Albina.

I know it was I alone that worked their ruin, 60
that from the throne, which his blood claimed for him,
Britannicus saw his hopes by me cast down.
Deprived, by me, of marrying Octavia,
the brother of Junia chose to abandon life.
That was Silanus, whom Claudius had marked out 65
for glory, whose great-grandfather was Augustus.
Nero enjoys all; and in recompense
I must hold the balance between them and him,
so that one day Britannicus may hold it,
with the same justice, between my son and me. 70

Albina

What scheme!

Agrippina

              I assure myself a port in the storm.
If this curb does not hold him, Nero escapes me.

Albina

But to take such precautions against a son!

Agrippina

I should soon fear him if he stopped fearing me.

Albina

Perhaps you fear unjustly. But if Nero 75
is now, for you, no longer what he should be,
at least we have heard no rumor of his change,
and these are secrets between Caesar and you.
Whatever proud new title Rome accords him,
he gives it to his mother. His graciousness 80
is prodigal, keeps nothing for himself:
your name, in all Rome, is as sacred as his;
one almost never speaks of sad Octavia.
Your grandfather Augustus gave less honor
to Livia. Nero is the first to allow 85
the laureled fasces to precede his mother.
What proofs do you require of his gratitude?

Agrippina

A little less respect, more confidence.
Albina, all these presents excite my loathing:
I see my honors grow and my credit fall. 90
No, no, the time is past when, still a boy,

he would turn toward me the praises of his court,
when he trusted me to govern, when my order
would bring the senate to the palace, and I
behind a veil—invisible, present—would be   95
of that great body the all-powerful soul.
Unsure, then, of Rome's will, he was not yet
intoxicated with his grandeur. That day,
that sad day I remember when suddenly
his own fame dazzled him. The ambassadors   100
of various kings had come to recognize him
in the world's name. I went to place myself
beside him, on his throne. I do not know
whose counsel prompted my humiliation.
No matter. Nero, at his first sight of me,   105
let his displeasure show in his countenance.
My heart knew it for omen. The thankless one,
glossing his insult over with sham respect,
stood up too soon and, running to embrace me,
led me aside from my intended place.   110
Since that unlucky stroke, Agrippina's power
from day to day draws quickly to its end.
Only the shadow is left me: now all implore
the name of Seneca, the support of Burrus.

Albina

But if your soul is warned by this suspicion,   115
why do you nurse the venom that kills you? Deign,
at least, to have an understanding with Caesar.

Agrippina

He no longer sees me without witnesses.
In public, at my appointed hour, I am heard.
His answer, even his silence, is dictated.   120
I now see two observers, his masters and mine,
preside, one or the other, at all our meetings.
And yet the more he runs, the more I'll pursue.
I must profit by his troubled conscience, Albina.
I hear a sound: they are opening. Let us go in   125
boldly, at once, to challenge this abduction.
Let us surprise, if we can, his inmost thoughts.
But what . . . already Burrus leaves him?

(Enter Burrus.)

Burrus
                              Madam,
in the Emperor's name I was coming to announce
an order that might at first alarm you, but one   130
that is only the effect of a prudent course
Caesar would have explained to you.
Agrippina
                              Since he would,
let us go in: he will explain it better.
Burrus
Caesar has for some time withdrawn from our sight.
Already the two consuls, by a door   135
less known to the public, have preceded you.
But, madam, permit me to return expressly—
Agrippina
No, I will not disturb his lofty secrets.
But are you willing, meanwhile, that we two,
more candid, speak for once without pretense?   140
Burrus
Burrus has always too much hated falsehood—
Agrippina
How long do you propose to hide the Emperor?
Am I to see him only as an intruder?
Have I then lifted up your fortune so high
that you might barricade my son from me?   145
Dare you not risk him a moment to himself?
Do Seneca and you compete for the glory
of effacing me the sooner from his mind?
Have I trusted him to you to make him scorn me?
That you, in his name, should be masters of the State?   150
Indeed, the more I reflect upon it, the less
I can believe you dared to think me your creature:
you whose ambition I could have let grow old,
decked in some legion's obscure honors, and I
who followed my ancestors upon the throne—   155
daughter, wife, sister, mother of your masters.
Then what do you propose? Do you think I have made
one emperor, to put three above me? Nero

67

is a child no longer. Is it not time he reigned?
Until what day would you have the Emperor fear you? 160
Can he see nothing but through your borrowed eyes?
Has he not, in short, his ancestors to guide him?
Let him choose Augustus, Tiberius, if he will,
or Germanicus my father, if he can.
I dare not place myself among such heroes; 165
but there are virtues I can point out: at least
I can show him how much distance, when placing trust,
to keep between a subject and himself.

Burrus

I had only been concerned on this occasion
with excusing Caesar for a single act; 170
but since, without wishing me to justify him,
you make me answer for the rest of his life,
I will reply with the liberty of a soldier
unskilled in coloring the truth. You, madam,
I own, entrusted Caesar's youth to me. 175
My constant duty is to remember this.
But did I swear to betray him, to make of him
an emperor with no skill but to obey?
No. It is not to you I must answer now.
He is your son no longer, he is the master 180
of the world. My accounting, madam, is to Rome,
the empire, which sees his welfare in my hands.
If one had wished to rear him in ignorance,
was there none to do it but Seneca and me?
Why chase the flatterers from his guardian crew? 185
Why bring corruptors back from exile?* The court
of Claudius, teeming with slaves, would have supplied
a thousand for each two required, all begging
for the honor of degrading him: in a long
infancy they would have let him grow old. 190
What is your grievance, madam? You are revered.
One swears by Caesar's mother as by Caesar.
The Emperor, it is true, no longer comes
each day to bring the empire's homage, to throng

---

* Seneca, exiled in Corsica by Messalina, had been recalled by Agrippina to be one of Nero's tutors.

your court. But must he? Can his gratitude   195
be shown only by his dependence? Still
humble, still the shy Nero, must he dare
to be Augustus and Caesar only in name?
Would you know all I think? Rome justifies him.
Rome, to three former slaves so long enslaved,   200
still scarcely lightened of the yoke it wore,
now dates its liberty from the reign of Nero.
Yes, even virtue seems reborn. No longer
is the whole empire plunder to one who rules.
The people, crowding the Martian field, elect   205
their magistrates; Caesar appoints the chiefs
at the soldiers' bidding; Thrasea in the senate,
Corbulo in the army, despite their fame,
are honest still; the island wildernesses,
once rife with senators, are now the abode   210
only of their denunciators. What matter
if he still listens to us, provided this
tends to his glory and, through a flourishing reign,
Rome is still free and Caesar omnipotent?
But, madam, Nero is ready for self-guidance.   215
I obey, without presuming to teach. No doubt
he has only to abide by his ancestors;
to do well, he has only to be himself:
fortunate if his virtues, strongly conjoined,
renew, each year, the likeness of his first years.   220

Agrippina

So, mistrustful of the future, you believe
Nero will lose his way without you. But you
who, for the present satisfied with your work,
have just maintained his virtues, will you now
tell us why Nero, become a ravisher,   225
takes forcibly the sister of Silanus?
Is it merely his desire to humiliate
my ancestral blood that shines in Junia? Of what
does he accuse her? How has she become,
in one day, a state criminal—she who, reared   230
without ambitious pride, would never have seen
Nero, but that he had her taken by force:

she would even have counted among his favors
the high good fortune of never seeing him?
Burrus
    I know she is not suspected of any crime,   235
but as yet, madam, Caesar has not condemned her.
Here there is nothing to offend her eyes:
she is in a palace filled with her ancestors.
You know the rights inherent in her birth
could make her husband a rebellious prince;   240
you know the blood of Caesar must be allied
only with those to whom he freely trusts it;
and you yourself will own, it would not be fair
to dispose of her, one of Augustan race,
without his knowledge.   245
Agrippina
                I see: he tells me, through you,
Britannicus looks vainly to my choice.
Vainly, to turn his eyes from his wretchedness,
I let him build his hopes upon this marriage.
To mortify me, Nero would have it seen
that Agrippina's promise exceeds her power.   250
Rome takes my influence too much for granted:
by this affront he would have the Romans know
their false assumption, the world learn, with terror,
not to confuse the emperor with my son.
He well may do it. But still I dare to warn him   255
that, before this hardy stroke, he should make firm
his sovereign power: that, in requiring me
to test my poor authority against him,
he risks his own, and in the balance my name
may have more weight than he assumes.   260
Burrus
                      What, madam!
Forever doubting his respect? Can he
not take one step but that you find it devious?
Does the Emperor know you are supporting Junia?
That you are reconciled with Britannicus?
Do you become the prop of your enemies   265
that you may find some pretext for blaming Caesar?

Will you be always ready to disunite
the empire, at the least rumor that comes your way?
Will you fear constantly? Will your embraces
stand upon explanations? Come, lay by   270
the mournful diligence of a censor; affect
the indulgence of a mild forgiving mother;
permit some differences without airing them,
and do not tempt the court to abandon you.

Agrippina

Who would be honored by Agrippina's support   275
when Nero himself gives notice of my ruin,
when from his presence he seems to banish me—
when Burrus dares to stop me at his door?

Burrus

It is clear, madam, that I had best be silent
and that my liberty begins to offend.   280
The grieved heart is unjust: all arguments
that do not flatter it deepen its suspicions.
Here is Britannicus. I make way for him,
that you may hear the story of his disgrace
and pity it—and perhaps, madam, accuse   285
those whom the Emperor has consulted least.

        (*Exit Burrus. Enter Britannicus and Narcissus.*)

Agrippina

Ah! Prince, where are you going? What ardor, what dread
propel you blindly among your enemies?
What are you seeking?

Britannicus

               What am I seeking? Gods!
All I have lost, madam, is here. Walled round   290
by maniples of frightening soldiers, Junia
has been abominably haled to this palace.
O wretched thing! To one of her shy nature,
the horrible surprise of that strange sight!
At last she is taken from me. A brutal power   295
now separates two hearts joined by misfortune.
No doubt it is not permitted that, sharing our griefs,
we help each other to endure them.

Agrippina
>   Enough.
Like you, I take your injuries to heart:
my protests have anticipated your own;   300
but I will not pretend that a futile anger
redeems my promise and pays my debt to you.
No more at present. If you would understand me,
come to the house of Pallas. I shall wait there.
>   (*Exeunt Agrippina and Albina.*)

Britannicus
Shall I believe her, Narcissus? Should I trust her   305
as arbiter between her son and me?
Tell me, is she not Agrippina still,
whom once my father married, to his ruin,
and who, if I believe you, hastened the course
of his last days, too slow for her designs?   310

Narcissus
No matter. She feels herself, as much as you,
outraged: she has determined to give you Junia.
Unite your grievances; combine your interests.
This palace echoes vainly with your regrets;
while you are seen here making humble protests,   315
sowing about you, not terror, but complaint,
while your resentments lose themselves in words,
be sure of it: you will protest forever.

Britannicus
Ah, but you know, Narcissus, whether I mean
to keep much longer the habit of servitude—   320
whether, stunned by my downfall, I renounce
my destiny, the empire, for all time.
But I am still alone. My father's friends
are now so many strangers, cold to my misery;
my very youth keeps far from me all those   325
who in their hearts are loyal. As for myself,
during a year in which some slight experience
has made me realize my unhappy lot,
whom do I see about me but venal friends,
assiduous watchers of my every movement,   330
who, chosen by Nero for this infamous trade,

now traffic in my private thoughts with him?
However it may be, I am daily sold:
he sees my plans, he hears my conversations;
like you, he knows the currents of my heart.   335
What do you think, Narcissus?

Narcissus

     Ah, what baseness!
It is for you to choose discreet companions,
my lord, and not to throw your secrets away.

Britannicus

Well said. But this unreadiness to trust
is always the last science of a great heart: 340
it is long duped. But I believe you now.
Indeed I swear to believe no one else.
My father, I recall, vouched for your zeal.
You alone, of his freedmen, are constant to me;
your eyes, incessantly upon my course,   345
have saved me from a thousand hidden reefs.
Go, then: see if the rumor of this new storm
wakens the courage of our friends. Look well
into their eyes, take note of every word;
see what the chances are of their loyal aid.   350
Above all, in this palace, adroitly mark
how closely Nero keeps the Princess guarded.
Know if the light of danger has left her eyes,
and whether I may see her. Meanwhile I go
to the house of Pallas, my father's freedman like you,   355
to speak with Nero's mother. I'll edge her anger,
join in her schemes—if possible, set afoot,
under her name, even more than she intends.

ACT TWO

(Enter Nero, Burrus, Narcissus, and guards.)

Nero

Make no mistake, Burrus: unjust as she is,
she is my mother. I will ignore her caprices.   360
But I will neither ignore nor tolerate
the insolent minister who dares to abet them.
Pallas feeds her the poison of his advice;
he daily subverts Britannicus my brother.
They listen to him alone: go after them   365
and you would probably find them at his house.
Enough of this. I must remove him from both.
For the last time, let him be off, let him go.
I wish, I order it; at the end of day
let me not find him in Rome or in my court.   370
Go, Burrus: this concerns the empire's safety.

(Exit Burrus.)

You, Narcissus, approach.
    (To the guards)
            And you, retire.

(Exeunt guards.)

Narcissus

The Gods be thanked, with Junia in your hands
you can be sure, sir, of all other Romans.
Your enemies, cast down from their vain hope,   375
at the house of Pallas weep for their helplessness.
But now what do I see? You yourself, unquiet,
distraught, seem more alarmed than Britannicus.
What does this frowning sadness portend to me,
these somber glances roving without aim?   380
All smiles upon you: fortune obeys your will.

Nero

No use, Narcissus. Nero is in love.

74

Narcissus
  You?
Nero
      For a moment past, but for all my life.
  I love—what am I saying?—I worship Junia.
Narcissus
  You love her?
Nero
              Stirred by a curious desire,   385
  last night when she arrived, I went to see her
  led in—sad, raising to heaven her tear-wet eyes,
  which shone among the torches and flashing arms:
  beautiful without gauds, in the simple dress
  of a lovely woman just uprooted from sleep.   390
  How explain it? I do not know if this negligence,
  the flares, the shadows, the outcries and the silence,
  the unfeeling aspect of her rude abductors,
  heightened the timid sweetness of her look.
  However it may be, I was ravished. I stood   395
  wishing to speak to her, and my voice had left me:
  unmoving, held by a long astonishment,
  I let her pass me, into her private rooms.
  I went to mine. It was there, in solitude,
  I attempted vainly to throw off her image: 400
  she was too clear, too present. I thought we spoke;
  I loved even the tears I caused to flow.
  Sometimes I asked her pardon, but too late;
  I entreated her with sighs, even with threats.
  Thus, rapt in contemplation of my new love,   405
  my eyes wide open, I awaited the light.
  And yet perhaps I imagine her too fair;
  she appeared before me to undue advantage,
  would you not say, Narcissus?
Narcissus
                  Sir, how believe
  she could have hidden herself so long from Nero?   410
Nero
  You know quite well. Whether her anger blamed me
  for the misfortune of her brother's death,

or whether, clinging to an austere pride,
she grudged her nascent beauty to our sight,
deeply secluded, faithful to her sorrow,   415
she lived in hiding even from her renown.
It is this virtue, so novel at the court,
whose perseverance excites my love. How rare,
Narcissus! While there is not a Roman girl
my longing would not honor and leave more vain,   420
none who, when first grown confident of her eyes,
would not come flying to test them upon Caesar,
only the modest Junia, in her palace,
regards their honors as a stigma, avoids us,
and does not deign, perhaps, to inform herself   425
if I am worthy of love, or able to love.
Tell me: Britannicus cares for her?
Narcissus

                              What, sir!

You ask?
Nero

              So young still—does he know himself?
Does he know the fatal sorcery of a look?
Narcissus

Love still comes before reason, sir. Be sure,   430
he is in love. Instructed by such beauty,
his eyes already are accustomed to tears.
He has learned to acquiesce in her least desire;
perhaps already he has learned to persuade.
Nero

You tell me he has some command of her heart?   435
Narcissus

I do not know; but, sir, I can tell you this:
at times I have seen him fling out of this palace,
full of a rage he hid from you, hurt deeply
by the ingratitude of a court that shuns him,
sick of your greatness and of his servitude,   440
yet vacillating between impatience and fear:
he would go to Junia, and return content.
Nero

The worse for him if he has attracted her,

Narcissus; he had rather wish for her anger.
Nero will not be jealous without revenge.   445

Narcissus

You? And why, sir, should you be apprehensive?
She may have pitied him and shared his distress;
she has looked upon no suffering but his.
But when her eyes, today unsealed, beholding
at closer range the brilliance with which you shine,   450
observe about you the kings undiademed,
unnoted in the crowd, and her lover himself,
all watching you for the honor of a glance
you may let fall at random: when she sees
you, at this pitch of glory, come before her,   455
sighing, acknowledging her victory, then—
master, doubt not, of a heart already charmed—
command that love shall follow. You will be loved.

Nero

How many torments I must be prepared for,
what tiresome interference!

Narcissus

                       Why, sir, what stops you?   460

Nero

All stops me. Octavia, Agrippina, Burrus,
Seneca. All of Rome. Three years of virtue.
Not that the least scrap of affection holds me
to Octavia now, or makes me pity her youth.
Too long fatigued by her solicitous ways,   465
I rarely deign to notice her melancholy.
What luck if the quick favor of a divorce
relieved me of a yoke that was forced upon me!
Even heaven, secretly, seems to condemn her;
four years her prayers have badgered it; the Gods   470
let fall no hint that her virtue touches them:
they give no promise to her womb, Narcissus;
vainly the empire clamors for an heir.

Narcissus

Why do you wait, sir, to repudiate her—
decried by the empire, by your heart, by all?   475
Your ancestor Augustus sighed for Livia;

77

they were united by a double divorce,
and to this happy breach you owe the empire.
Tiberius, married into his family, dared
to repudiate his daughter before his eyes.   480
You alone, still at odds with your desires,
dare not, by a divorce, make certain of joy.

Nero

Do you not know the implacable Agrippina?
My anxious love already imagines her
leading Octavia here, and, eyes aflame,   485
attesting the sanctity of a knot she tied—
then, for my further punishment, delivering
a long recital of my thankless deeds.
How face that wretched interview?

Narcissus

                              Are you not
your master, sir, and hers? Are we to see you   490
forever trembling under her tutelage?
Now live, reign, for yourself. You have reigned for her
too much. Do you fear . . . but, sir, you do not fear her:
you have just banished the overweening Pallas,
whose insolence you know she encourages.   495

Nero

Far from her eyes, I give commands, make threats,
I listen to your counsel, I dare to approve.
I excite myself against her and try to rebel.
But (now I expose to you my naked soul)
when my misfortune brings me into her sight,   500
either I dare not yet deny the power
of eyes where I have read my duty so long,
or, faithful to so much beneficence,
my memory, in secret, admits what I owe:
at all events, my efforts go for nothing,   505
my daunted genius trembles before hers.
It is to free myself from this dependence
that I avoid her, that I even abuse her,
and from time to time exasperate her woes,
that, as I fly from her, she may fly from me.   510

But I am keeping you. Retire, Narcissus:
Britannicus might well accuse you of craft.
Narcissus
No, no, Britannicus relies upon me.
He thinks I am seeing you at his command,
that I inquire into all that touches him.   515
He would learn your secrets from my mouth. Impatient
now, above all, to see his love again,
he expects this faithful help of my diligence.
Nero
I grant it. Take him this sweet news: he shall see her.
Narcissus
Sir, separate them. Banish him.
Nero
                        Narcissus,   520
I have my reasons; you may well suppose
I shall sell dear the pleasure of seeing her.
Boast to him, meanwhile, that your stratagem works:
say I am hoodwinked, that he is having his tryst
without my leave.—The doors part: she is coming.   525
Go to rejoin your master and bring him here.
                     (Exit Narcissus. Enter Junia.)
You are troubled, madam; your expression changes.
Do you read some sad foreboding in my eyes?
Junia
Sir, I will not conceal my error from you:
I was going to see Octavia, not the Emperor.   530
Nero
I know. I could not without envy learn
how kind you are to fortunate Octavia.
Junia
You, sir?
Nero
            Do you think, madam, within these walls,
none but Octavia is aware of you?
Junia
And whom, sir, do you wish me to implore?   535
Whom shall I ask to name my unknown crime?

You know it, you who punish it. I beg you,
tell me the nature of my lawless deeds.

Nero

What, madam? Is it then a light offense
to have hidden yourself from me so long? Those treasures   540
with which heaven wished to make you beautiful,
have you received them only to bury them?
Shall lucky Britannicus see undisturbed,
far from our eyes, the ripening of your charms?
Why, to this day excluded from that glory,   545
have I been sternly exiled in my court?
I have heard more: that when he dares to unfold
his thoughts to you, you endure it unoffended.
For I will not believe that the strict Junia,
without consulting me, would encourage his hopes,   550
or permit herself to love and to be loved
while I know nothing but what is noised abroad.

Junia

Sir, I shall not deny, he has been pleased
at times to show me his desires. He has not
turned from a solitary child, surviving   555
the ruin of an illustrious family.
He may remember that in a happier time
his father named me to receive his promise.
He loves me; he is obedient to the emperor
his father, and I dare say, to your mother.   560
Your own desires accord so much with hers—

Nero

My mother has her projects and I have mine.
Let us speak here no further, madam, of Claudius
and Agrippina: their choice is not my law.
I am responsible for you. I will choose   565
your husband at my own discretion.

Junia

                      Ah, sir,
do you reflect that any marriage but this
would shame the Caesars who have given me life?

Nero

No, the husband I propose to you can join

your ancestors without shame to his own: 570
you may unblushingly accept his love.
Junia
    And who, sir, is this husband?
Nero

                    Madam, I.

Junia
    You?
Nero
        I would give you, madam, another name
    if I knew any above Nero. Indeed,
    to offer you a choice you could ratify,   575
    I have surveyed the court, home, and the empire.
    The more I have sought, the more I continue to seek
    in what hands I should put this treasure, the more
    it appears that Caesar, alone worthy of you,
    should be himself the fortunate custodian,   580
    that he should trust you to no hands but these
    where Rome has placed the empire of mankind.
    Reflect, you too, upon your early years.
    Claudius had intended you for his son;
    but that was in a time when he thought to name him,   585
    one day, his imperial heir. The Gods have spoken.
    Rather than contradict them, it is for you
    to place yourself upon the empire's side.
    They would have honored me with this gift in vain
    if your heart must be separated from it—   590
    if such cares are not solaced by your beauty,
    and through these days of vigils and alarms,
    days always to be pitied and always envied,
    I do not find some respite at your feet.
    Let not Octavia disconcert you: Rome,   595
    as much as I, gives you its suffrage, rejects
    Octavia, tells me to dissolve a marriage
    heaven does not wish to recognize. Think well,
    ponder upon this choice, how worthy it is
    of the devoted zeal of a prince who loves you,   600
    of your own splendid eyes, too long immured,
    and of the world to which you owe yourself.

Junia

My lord, with reason I am left amazed.
I see myself, within a single day,
brought like a criminal to these premises,   605
and when I appear before you, much afraid,
hardly relying upon my innocence,
you abruptly offer me Octavia's place.
I have deserved, however, I dare protest,
neither this undue honor nor that affront.   610
How can you wish, my lord, that one who saw,
almost at birth, her family destroyed,
who, grieving in obscurity, has led
a virtuous life in keeping with her sorrow,
should suddenly emerge from this deep night   615
into a rank exposed to the world's eyes,
whose bright gaze, from afar, I could not meet,
and where another woman supremely reigns?

Nero

I repudiate her. I have told you as much.
Have less anxiety or less modesty.   620
Do not accuse my choice of blindness; I answer
for you and for the outcome: merely consent.
Recall the blood from which your life proceeds;
and to the solid glory of those honors
Caesar would give you, do not prefer the glory   625
of one refusal, subject to remorse.

Junia

Sir, heaven can look into my inmost thought.
I set no store by an extravagant fame;
I see the greatness of this rank you would give me,
but the more splendor it might cast, the deeper   630
my shame would be, the more apparent my crime
of having taken it from its rightful heir.

Nero

This is to be most thoughtful of her interests.
Friendship can go no further. But let us not
flatter ourselves, and let us drop the mystery.   635
The sister touches you much less than the brother;
and for Britannicus—

82

Junia
                    Indeed he has touched me.
I have not hidden it. This sincerity
may well be indiscretion, but my mouth
is always the interpreter of my heart.   640
I, absent from the court, have had no reason
to think that I should practice the art of feigning.
I love Britannicus. I was promised to him
when the succession waited upon his marriage.
But the misfortunes that deprived him of it,   645
his honors gone, his palace empty, the flight
of a court alienated by his fall,
these are so many ties to assure my love.
All that you see conspires to do your will;
your cloudless days go by in pleasures. For you   650
the empire is their inexhaustible source;
or if they are interrupted by some chagrin,
the whole world, bent upon their smooth continuance,
tries eagerly to efface it from your mind.
Britannicus is alone. Whatever afflicts him,   655
he has none but me to show concern, no pleasure
but in the consolation of a few tears
that bring release, at times, from his troubled thoughts.
Nero
It is these pleasures and these tears I envy,
for which another would pay me with his life;   660
but for this prince I know a gentler treatment.
Madam, he will appear before you soon.
Junia
Ah, sir, I have always trusted in your virtues!
Nero
I could have barred his access to this place;
but, madam, I would anticipate the danger   665
his vengefulness might court. No, I would not
work his undoing. Better that he himself
should hear his sentence from the mouth he loves.
If you much prize his safety, send him off,
yet give him no occasion to think me jealous.   670
Let the offense of his banishment be yours;

and either by your words or by your silence,
at least by your cold manner, make him know
he must take elsewhere his desires and hopes.

Junia

I? That I should pronounce so cruel a judgment!   675
A thousand times I have sworn the contrary.
But even if my lips could play me false,
my eyes, sir, would command him to disobey.

Nero

Hidden close by, I shall observe you, madam.
Lock up your fondness in your deepest soul.   680
You will have no secret languages from me:
those looks you think are mute will be understood,
and his death be the infallible reward
of a gesture or a sigh that may escape you
to reassure him.   685

Junia

        Alas, if I still dare
to express a wish, let me not see him again!

                             (*Enter Narcissus.*)

Narcissus

Britannicus, my lord, asks for the Princess.
He is coming.

Nero

        Let him come.

Junia

             Ah, sir!

Nero

                   I leave you.
His fortune rests with you more than with me.
Seeing him, madam, reflect that I see you.   690

                             (*Exit Nero.*)

Junia

Ah, dear Narcissus, head your master back!
Tell him. . . . I am lost. He is already here.

                     (*Enter Britannicus.*)

Britannicus

Madam, what luck brings me to you? Is it so?
I have the blessed chance of speaking with you?

But at the moment of this pleasure, what grief   695
consumes me! Can I hope to see you again?
Must I take stealthily, with a thousand wiles,
a happiness you daily granted? What night,
what waking! Did not your tears, did not your presence
disarm the insolence of those cruel men?   700
What was your lover doing? What envious demon
grudged me the honor of dying before your eyes?
Alas, in the sudden fear that came upon you,
did you, in secret, cry to me? My Princess,
were you so generous as to wish for me?   705
Did you imagine how I should suffer for you?
You do not speak? Is this my welcome? What coldness!
Is this your solace for my disgrace? Reply.
We are alone. Our enemy, deceived,
while I am speaking to you, is elsewhere engaged.   710
Let us be quick to use this lucky absence.

Junia

You are within a sanctum of his power.
These very walls, sir, may have eyes; the Emperor
is never absent from this place.

Britannicus

               Since when,
madam, are you so fearful? What is this?   715
Your love so soon becomes a willing subject?
Where is the heart that always swore to me
we should make even Nero envy our love?
But, madam, cast away an idle fear.
Loyalty is not dead in every heart;   720
all, by their look, seem to approve my anger;
the mother of Nero has declared for us,
and Rome itself, offended by his conduct—

Junia

Ah, sir, you speak against your own conviction!
You yourself have acknowledged a thousand times   725
that Rome acclaimed him with a common voice;
you have always paid some tribute to his virtue.
No doubt your sorrow moves you to this speech.

85

Britannicus

These arguments surprise me, I must confess.
I did not seek you out to hear him praised.   730
To tell you of my grave anxiety,
I seize, with effort, a favorable moment,
and this slight precious time, madam, is used
in praising the enemy who persecutes me.
What makes you, in one day, so unlike yourself?   735
Even your eyes have learned to reveal nothing?
What do I see? You dare not meet my own?
Can Nero please you? Is my presence hateful?
Ah, if I thought so. . . . Madam, in the Gods' name,
resolve this turmoil into which you cast me.   740
Speak. Have you quite effaced me from your mind?

Junia

Retire, my lord. The Emperor soon returns.

Britannicus

After this blow, Narcissus, whom shall I trust?

> *(Exit Britannicus. Enter Nero.)*

Nero

Madam—

Junia

> No, nothing more; I can hear nothing.
You are obeyed, sir. Now permit at least   745
the flowing of tears he will not see.

> *(Exit Junia.)*

Nero

> Ah, well!
You observe the violence of their love, Narcissus;
it was apparent even in her silence.
She loves my rival, it cannot be ignored;
but I shall be delighted to dash his hopes.   750
I find the image of his grief enchanting,
and I have seen him doubt her sincerity.
I follow her. He awaits you, to pour forth
his anguish. Go and stab him with new suspicions;
and while I see her lamenting, adoring him,   755
let him pay well for his unknown good luck.

> *(Exit Nero.)*

86

Narcissus (alone)
Fortune calls you a second time, Narcissus;
would you resist her voice? No, let us follow
even to the end her favorable orders,
and, to be happy, ruin unhappy men. 760

ACT THREE

(*Enter Nero and Burrus.*)

Burrus
    Sir, Pallas will obey.
Nero
                        And what effect
    upon my mother, to see his pride confounded?
Burrus
    Sir, do not doubt, this is a blow to her,
    and soon her pain will burst into reproaches.
    Her fits of anger have long been unconcealed: 765
    if only they might end with futile cries!
Nero
    You think her capable of some intrigue?
Burrus
    Sir, Agrippina is still dangerous. Rome
    and all your soldiers revere her ancestors;
    Germanicus her father is present to them.   770
    She knows her power; you know her intrepid heart;
    and what, to me, makes her more formidable
    is that you lend support to her indignation
    and furnish her with arms against yourself.
Nero
    I, Burrus?
Burrus
                    This love, sir, that possesses you—   775
Nero
    I understand you, Burrus. The case is hopeless.
    My heart has blamed itself more than you blame it.
    All said, I am bound to love.
Burrus
                            You imagine this,
    my lord: content with offering some resistance,
    you let an evil, in its beginning slight,   780

88

unnerve you. But if your heart, held to its duty,
decided to make no terms with its enemy,
if you considered the glory of your first years,
if you were pleased, sir, to recall the virtues
of Octavia, worthy of a better prize,   785
her chaste affection rising above your scorn;
above all, if your eyes, avoiding Junia,
were self-condemned to some few days of absence,
believe me, powerful as the charm may be,
we do not love except by wishing to love.   790

Nero

I shall believe you, Burrus, when among dangers
the glory of our arms must be upheld,
or when, more tranquil, seated in the senate,
I must resolve the destiny of the State;
then I shall put my trust in your experience.   795
But love, believe me, is a different science,
and I should be reluctant to impose
your stern ideas upon these lesser things.
Adieu. I am too much grieved, away from Junia.

                                                    (*Exit Nero.*)

Burrus (*alone*)

So, Burrus, at last, Nero reveals his nature.   800
That which you thought to curb, that ferocity,
is ready to break free from your feeble bonds.
In what excesses it well may lash abroad!
O Gods! At this dark omen, what course to take?
Seneca, who should help me, has other cares,   805
is far from Rome, knows nothing of this danger.
What then? If, by softening Agrippina's heart,
I could. . . . She is here; my luck brings her to me.

                            (*Enter Agrippina and Albina.*)

Agrippina

Well! I was wrong in my suspicions, Burrus?
You prove yourself with some illustrious lessons!   810
Pallas is being exiled—whose crime, perhaps,
is to have put your master upon the throne.
How well you know it: Claudius, whom he counseled,
would never, but for him, have adopted my son.

What more? His wife is given a rival: Nero   815
is freed from the marriage promise. Worthy task
of a minister at war with flatterers, chosen
to hold in leash his youthful passions: fine work,
to flatter them himself, to induce in him
scorn for his mother, unconcern for his wife!   820

Burrus

You accuse too quickly, madam. Every act
of the Emperor, to this point, can be justified.
In the case of Pallas, admit necessity:
his pride has long demanded this punishment;
the Emperor simply carries out, with regret,   825
what the whole court urged secretly. The other
is a misfortune not without relief:
Octavia's weeping can be checked at the source.
But calm your anger. In a gentler way
you can restore her husband sooner to her: 830
threats, furious words, will lead his cruelty on.

Agrippina

What a vain hope, to try to shut my mouth!
My silence, it is clear, wins your contempt;
nor will I cower before my own creation.
Not all of Agrippina's support flies   835
with Pallas: heaven leaves me enough for vengeance.
The son of Claudius is beginning to feel
those wrongs which gained me nothing but remorse.
I will show him, have no doubt, to the army, deplore
his oppressed childhood to the soldiers, cause them   840
to expiate their error as I do mine.
On one side they will see the son of an emperor,
claiming the homage sworn to his family,
and hear the daughter of Germanicus—
on the other side, Ahenobarbus' son,   845
upheld by Seneca and the tribune Burrus,
who, called from exile by myself, now share,
before my eyes, the sovereignty. I intend
that they shall learn the truth of our common crimes:
they'll know by what paths I have guided him.   850
To assure their hatred of his power and yours,

I will confirm the most injurious rumors,
confess to all: exiles, assassinations,
poison itself. . . .
Burrus
        They'll not believe you, madam.
They will be quick to challenge the sly game   855
of a revengeful witness self-accused.
For my part, I, who first took up your plans,
who even swore the army to his cause,
do not repent that single-hearted faith.
This, madam, is a son succeeding his father.   860
In adopting Nero, Claudius by design
confused the rights of his son and your own.
Rome, then, could choose him. Thus, without prejudice,
it chose Tiberius, stepson of Augustus;
and young Agrippa, descendant of his blood,   865
saw barred to him the vainly asserted rank.
Fixed upon such examples, Nero's power
cannot be weakened, now, by you yourself;
and if he hears me still, madam, his goodness
will soon persuade you to abandon the wish.   870
I have begun my task. I will carry on.
                              (*Exit Burrus.*)
Albina
Into what violence your resentment leads you,
madam! May such remarks not reach the Emperor.
Agrippina
Ah, let him only show his face to me!
Albina
Madam, in the Gods' name, conceal your anger.   875
What? For the sister's or the brother's sake,
must you give up your peace and security?
Will you rule Caesar even in choice of loves?
Agrippina
So, then, you do not see how they let me down,
Albina? It is to me they give a rival.   880
Soon, if I do not break this dire attachment,
my place is occupied, I am nothing at all.
Octavia with her empty title, till now,

of no use to the court, was ignored by it.
Graces and honors, by me alone dispensed,   885
drew to me the self-seeking prayers of mortals.
Another has taken Caesar by surprise:
she'll have the authority of wife and mistress.
The end of so much striving, the pomp of the Caesars—
all will be hers if she but looks at him.   890
Why, see, he avoids me now. Already abandoned. . . .
Ah, Albina, I cannot bear the thought! Although
I should hasten the Gods' fatal judgment, Nero,
the ungrateful Nero. . . . But here his rival comes.

                  (*Enter Britannicus and Narcissus.*)

Britannicus

Our common enemies can still be opposed,   895
madam; our troubles find responsive hearts.
Your friends and mine, so secret once, while we
lost time in vain regrets, now burn with the wrath
injustice sets alight: they have lately shared
their grieved thoughts with Narcissus. Nero, as yet,   900
does not possess unchallenged the heartless one
whom in derision of my sister he loves.
If her ill use still touches you, the perjurer
may be restored to his duty. Half the senate
is mindful of our interests. Sulla, Piso,   905
Plautus—

Agrippina

           What are you saying, Prince? The leaders
of the nobility—Sulla, Piso, Plautus!

Britannicus

This news, I see, distresses you; your anger,
trembling, irresolute, already fears
to obtain all it wished. Fear nothing, madam.   910
You have too well established my disgrace;
no friend, be sure, will dare in my behalf.
I have none left: your too far-seeing efforts
long since corrupted or estranged them all.

Agrippina

My lord, give less belief to your suspicions: 915
our safety rests upon our will to agree.

I promised, that is enough. Let them oppose you,
I take back nothing I have promised. Nero,
guiltily, uselessly, runs from my anger.
Soon or late he must hear his mother speak.   920
I will try force and gentleness by turns;
or I will go myself, leading your sister,
to sow broadcast her consternation and mine,
rallying all hearts to her tears. Farewell.
I will lay siege to Nero on every hand.   925
You, if you trust me at all, keep from his sight.

(*Exeunt Agrippina and Albina.*)

Britannicus

Have you not flattered me with a false hope?
Can I take some assurance from what you say,
Narcissus?

Narcissus

       Yes. But, sir, this is not the place
to unfold that secret matter. Let us go.   930
Why are you waiting?

Britannicus

              Why do I wait, Narcissus?
Alas!

Narcissus

     Explain.

Britannicus

           If once more, by your skill,
I could see. . . .

Narcissus

       Whom?

Britannicus

              I blush for it—but then
I should more quietly wait my destiny.

Narcissus

You believe her faithful, after all I have said?   935

Britannicus

No, I believe her ungrateful, criminal,
deserving anger—but feel, despite myself,
I am not believing it as much as I should.
In its disorder my stubborn heart supplies

93

reasons for her, excuses her, worships her.   940
In short, I would conquer my incredulity
and hate her calmly. How believe a heart
so noble by all signs, so much at odds
with a false court since childhood, would renounce
that good fame—would contrive, from the first day,   945
a faithlessness without example at court?

Narcissus

And who can know if in her long retreat
the thankless girl has not been meditating
her conquest of the Emperor? Sure that her beauty
could not be hidden, perhaps she fled to be sought: 950
to excite Nero with the arduous glory
of taming a till-then-invincible pride.

Britannicus

So I am not to see her?

Narcissus

                              Sir, at this moment
she listens to the vows of her new lover.

Britannicus

Come, then. But what is this I see? She is here.   955

Narcissus (aside)

Ah, Gods! The Emperor must be told of this.

                    (*Exit Narcissus. Enter Junia.*)

Junia

Retire, my lord, and do not face an anger
my constancy of heart sets burning against you.
Nero is much provoked. While his mother was there
I stole away: she tries to detain him now.   960
Farewell; await, without offending my love,
the happy day that will see me justified.
You are always present to me: nothing can banish
your image from my mind.

Britannicus

                      I believe you, madam.
You would have me go, to make your hopes secure,   965
to leave an open field to your new ambition.
No doubt a secret shame at the sight of me

will let you taste only a troubled joy.
I must go, then.

Junia

                    My lord, without believing—

Britannicus

You should at least have struggled longer! I know   970
a common friendship hastens to the side
that fortune flatters. I do not complain
that the splendor of an empire could dazzle you,
that you would have it at my sister's expense,
but that, taken with these grandeurs like another,   975
you appeared so long to be untouched by them.
No, I must say again, my desperate heart
against this one disaster was not prepared.
I have seen injustice triumph above my ruin,
and heaven accomplice of my persecutors.   980
Not all those horrors had exhausted its wrath:
it remained for me to be forgotten by you.

Junia

My just impatience, in a happier time,
would make you sorry for your little faith.
But Nero threatens us: this danger at hand,   985
I have other cares, my lord, than to punish you.
Go, set your doubts at rest; complain no more:
Nero was listening. I was forced to pretend.

Britannicus

What! The cruel—

Junia

                    Close beside me, witness of all,
with a stern face was peering into my own,   990
ready to take his vengeance upon your life
for any sign of understanding between us.

Britannicus

Nero was listening, madam! But alas,
your eyes could have pretended, yet not deceived me.
They could have told me the author of that crime.   995
Is love mute? Has it no expression but words?
From what dismay one glance would have rescued me!
You needed only—

Junia

I needed to be still
and save you. How many times—since you must be told—
my heart all but informed you of its distress: 1000
how often I held back my sighs, avoided
your glance, which mine forever sought. What torment
to stand before a lover and not to speak,
to hear him plead and to afflict him still,
when one look would console him. But what tears   1005
that look would have set flowing! Aware of this,
anxious, confused, I did not think myself
inscrutable enough. I feared the pallor
of my shocked face; I thought my eyes must be
too full of misery. At each moment it seemed   1010
Nero was coming, in a tremendous rage,
to taunt me with my effort to reassure you.
I feared my love had been suppressed in vain;
I could have wished, at last, I had never loved.
Unfortunately for his peace, and ours,   1015
he is too well informed of both our hearts.
Once more, take leave: be hidden from his sight;
I will explain more clearly when there is time.
I have many other secrets.

Britannicus

These are too many:
it is too much, to make me realize   1020
my happiness, my wicked doubt, your goodness.
And do you know all you relinquish for me?
          (*Throwing himself at Junia's feet*)
When may I expiate this wrong at your feet?

Junia

What are you doing? Alas! Your rival comes.

                                        (*Enter Nero.*)

Nero

Prince, do continue these engaging raptures.   1025
I can conceive your favors by his thanks,
madam: I have just surprised him at your knees;
but to me, too, he has some thanks to render:

96

this place well suits him, and I keep you here
to make these tender assignations easier.   1030
Britannicus

  I can offer her my sorrow or my joy
wherever, in her goodness, she bids me welcome:
the aspect of this place where you hold her now
has nothing to astound me.
Nero

                    Has it not?
Does any glimpse of it not serve to warn you   1035
that I must be respected and obeyed?
Britannicus

  It did not see the two of us brought up,
I to obey you, you to challenge me.
When we were born, it did not think to hear
Domitius speak to me, one day, as a master.   1040
Nero

  Thus are our wishes crossed by destiny:
I was obedient then; now you obey.
Or if you are unprepared to accept guidance,
you are still young: being young, you may be taught.
Britannicus

  And who will teach me?
Nero

                The empire, with one voice: 1045
Rome.
Britannicus

      Does Rome arrogate among your rights
all cruelties of injustice and violence,
murders by poison, ravishment, divorce?
Nero

  Rome does not let its curious glances fall
upon those secrets I withhold from it.   1050
Imitate its respect.
Britannicus

      One knows what it thinks.
Nero

  At least it is silent; imitate its silence.

97

Britannicus

And so Nero begins to be quite free.

Nero

Nero begins to tire of your conversation.

Britannicus

All were disposed to bless his happy reign.   1055

Nero

Happy or not, they fear me. That is enough.

Britannicus

Such sentiments, if I know much of Junia,
will not deserve her praise.

Nero

                              At all events,
if I do not know the secret of pleasing her,
I have the art to punish an arrogant rival.   1060

Britannicus

As for myself, whatever danger befalls,
only her enmity could make me afraid.

Nero

Wish for it: that is all my advice to you.

Britannicus

Pleasing her is the only joy I wish.

Nero

She promised it to you: you will always please her.   1065

Britannicus

I could not think, at least, of spying upon her.
She may express herself in all that concerns me:
I do not wait in hiding to stop her speech.

Nero

I understand you. Guards!

                              (*Enter guards.*)

Junia

                    What are you doing?
This is your brother. He is in love. He is jealous.   1070
My lord, a thousand hardships beset his life.
How can his happiness excite your envy?
Consent that, drawing closer the bonds between you,
I hide myself from your eyes and from his.
My flight will end your fatal clashes. My lord,   1075

I will go join the company of vestals.
Grudge him no more my hapless vows: consent
that no one but the Gods be troubled by them.
Nero
The undertaking, madam, is strange and sudden.
Guards, let her be conducted to her rooms.   1080
Restrict Britannicus to those of his sister.
Britannicus
This is the way Nero contends for a heart.
Junia
Prince, let us not infuriate him but yield
before this storm.
Nero
                              Guards, do it without delay.
       (*Exeunt Britannicus and Junia, with guards. Enter Burrus.*)
Burrus
What's this? O heaven!
Nero (without seeing Burrus)
                                     So they burn twice as hot.   1085
I recognize the hand that brought them together.
When Agrippina announced herself and stood
stretching her conversation to such length,
it was only to bring off this odious meeting.
             (*Noticing Burrus*)
Let someone see if my mother is still about.   1090
Burrus, she is to remain here, under arrest.
Relieve her guard: let her be given mine.
Burrus
What! Sir, without hearing her? A mother?
Nero
                                                    Stop.
I do not know what scheme you are meditating,
Burrus, but for some time, whatever I wish,   1095
I find in you a censor ready to thwart me.
I say you shall answer to me for her. Refuse,
and others will—for her and for yourself.

ACT FOUR

(*Enter Agrippina and Burrus.*)

Burrus

    Yes, madam, you may freely defend yourself:
    Caesar grants you an audience here and now.   1100
    If by his order you were held at the palace,
    perhaps he had this conversation in mind.
    Whether he did or not, if I may be frank,
    give up the thought that he has offended you:
    prepare, rather, to meet him with open arms;   1105
    defend yourself, but do not accuse him, madam.
    The court, as you observe, looks only to him.
    Though still your son, and even your creation,
    he is your emperor. You are subject, like us,
    to this authority he received from you.   1110
    According as he may threaten or caress you,
    those of the court avoid you or run to your side;
    it is his support they seek in seeking yours.
    But now the Emperor comes.

Agrippina

                 Leave me with him.
           (*Exit Burrus. Enter Nero. She sits down.*)
    Approach, Nero, and take your place. I am told   1115
    to answer your suspicions. I do not know
    with what crime they have chosen to blacken me:
    I will inform you of all I have committed.
    You reign. You know what distance your birth put
    between you and the empire. Even the rights   1120
    of my ancestors, which Rome has consecrated,
    would not have served to bridge it, except for me.
    When the condemnation of Britannicus' mother
    left Claudius to be won, among so many
    beautiful women who intrigued for him,   1125

who sought his freedmen's backing, I coveted
his marriage bed with this one thought: to leave you
upon the throne where I should then be placed.
I curbed my pride; I went to solicit Pallas.
His master, day by day caressed in my arms,　　　　　　　　1130
found imperceptibly in the eyes of his niece
the love toward which I guided his tenderness.
But that relationship of blood between us
made Claudius shy at an incestuous match.
He dared not take the daughter of his brother.　　　　　　　1135
The senate was seduced: a more clement law
put Claudius in my bed, Rome at my knees.
This was much for myself; it was nothing for you.
I brought you with me into his family,
named you his son-in-law, gave you his daughter.　　　　　　1140
Silanus, who loved her, seeing himself cast off,
marked with his blood that unpropitious date.
Still it was nothing. Could you have hoped that Claudius
would prefer, one day, his son-in-law to his son?
I implored the ministry of Pallas again:　　　　　　　　　1145
Claudius, moved by his words, adopted you,
naming you Nero, and himself conferred
the sovereignty upon you before your time.
It was then that everyone, recalling the past,
saw my design, already too mature;　　　　　　　　　　1150
the coming downfall of Britannicus
called forth the protest of his father's friends.
A number of them I dazzled with promises;
exile delivered me from the most seditious;
Claudius himself, tired of my endless plaint,　　　　　　　1155
sequestered from his son those zealous minds,
long dedicated to serving his destiny,
that might reopen for him the way to the throne.
I did more: I appointed, from my suite,
those whom I wished to guide his course. For you,　　　　　1160
by a counter strategy, I was careful to name
tutors whom Rome with one consent admired.
I shut my ears to intrigue and believed renown.
I called from exile, I summoned from the army,

that very Seneca and that very Burrus   1165
who since. . . . Rome, at the time, esteemed their virtues.
Meanwhile, depleting the ample wealth of Claudius,
in your name I was spreading largess about:
spectacles, public gifts—invincible bait—
were drawing to you the people's, the soldiers', hearts,   1170
those who, besides, recalling their first love,
extolled in you my father Germanicus.
At this point Claudius was beginning to fail;
his eyes, long sealed, were opened at the end:
he knew his error. Absorbed in his dismay,   1175
he let some words of pity for his son
escape him; he wished, too late, to rally his friends.
I controlled all: his guards, his palace, his bed.
Letting him grieve his heart out fruitlessly,
I made myself the keeper of his last sighs: 1180
my attentions, apparently consoling him
while he was dying, hid his tears from his son.
He died. A thousand rumors, to my shame,
recount it. I withheld the news of his death.
While Burrus went obscurely to enjoin   1185
the army's pledge in your behalf, and you,
under my guard, were journeying to the camp,
in Rome the altars smoked with sacrifices;
by my false orders the whole excited people
prayed heaven to spare the prince already dead.   1190
At last, your power confirmed by the sworn vow
of all the legions, Claudius was shown forth:
the astonished people heard at the same time
of your imperial status and his death.
This is the frank confession I wished to make.   1195
These are my infamies. Here is my reward:
for scarcely six months did you seem to enjoy
the fruit of so much effort with gratitude,
when, tired of a respect that perhaps galled you,
you affected not to recognize me. I saw   1200
Burrus and Seneca, sharpening your suspicions,
ply you with lessons in disloyalty,
ravished to be excelled in their special skill.

I saw you favor with your confidence
Otho, Senecio—young voluptuaries,   1205
respectful flatterers of your every pleasure.
And when, your scorn exciting my reproach,
I called you to account for your insolence,
you answered in the one way the thankless know
who see themselves confounded: with new affronts.   1210
Now I am promising Junia to your brother;
both of them count upon your mother's choice:
what do you do? In one night, snatched to the court,
Junia becomes the object of your love.
I see Octavia quite forgotten, disposed   1215
to leave the marriage bed where I had placed her;
I see Pallas thrown out, your brother arrested;
you strike, at last, even at my freedom: Burrus
dares to lay his bold hands upon me. And when,
convicted of so many perfidies,   1220
you should have seen me only to expiate them,
it is you that order me to defend myself.

Nero

I remember always that I owe you the crown.
Rather than tire yourself with repeating this,
you, in your goodness, madam, with tranquil heart,   1225
might have been certain of my loyalty.
Moreover, those suspicions, those constant plaints,
made all who heard them believe (I say it here
between ourselves) that in the past you had worked,
under my name, entirely for your own ends.   1230
"So many honors," they said, "such marks of deference,
are these too slight rewards for her benefits?
What is the crime of this much rated son?
Has she exalted him that he might obey?
Is he the mere custodian of her power?"   1235
Not that, if even as such I could have pleased you,
I should not joyfully have yielded to you
this power you sought, apparently, to regain.
But Rome wishes a master, not a mistress.
You heard the common talk my weakness provoked.   1240
The senate, the people, daily irritated

to hear your whims command them through my voice,
were saying that Claudius, with his power, had left me
his foolish meekness too. A hundred times
you have seen our soldiers in a muttering rage   1245
carry their eagled staffs before you, ashamed
to mortify by that unworthy use
the heroes whose medallions are still upon them.
Another woman would have yielded to this,
but if you do not reign you are never content.   1250
Uniting with Britannicus against me,
you increase his strength with Junia's partisans,
and the hand of Pallas works at all these plots.
And when I am forced to make my peace secure,
I see you animated by spite and hate.   1255
You would present my rival to the army:
so goes the rumor, and it has reached the camp.

Agrippina

I, make him emperor, wretch? Did you believe it?
What would my purpose be? What could I have sought?
What honors in his court? What rank? If now,   1260
under your emperorship, I am spared nothing,
if my accusers watch my every step,
if they persist against their emperor's mother,
what would I do surrounded by a strange court?
They would reproach me, not with impotent cries,   1265
intentions stifled as soon as they are born,
but with crimes for you, committed in your sight,
for which only too soon I should be condemned.
You do not fool me; I know all your shifts:
you are ungrateful and you always were.   1270
From your first years, my attentions and my love
drew from you only a false show of caresses.
Nothing could conquer you; and your hard grain
should have deterred my kindness at the start.
How miserable I am! By what ill chance   1275
must all my efforts make me importunate?
I have no other son. O heaven, my witness,
have I said any prayer that was not for him?
Remorse, fear, dangers—nothing held me back;

I rose above his scorn; I turned my eyes   1280
from evils then foretold to me; I have done
all I could do: you reign, it is enough.
Now with my freedom, which you have stolen from me,
if you would have it, take my life as well,
provided the whole nation, stirred by my death,   1285
does not take from you what has cost so much.

Nero

Ah, well! Pass sentence. What would you have me do?

Agrippina

Punish the insolence of my accusers.
Compose the anger of Britannicus.
Let Junia take a husband of her choice.   1290
Let both of them be free. Let Pallas remain.
Give me permission to see you at all times—
            (*Perceiving Burrus at back of stage*)
let this same Burrus who comes to overhear us
not dare, in short, to stop me at your door.

Nero

Yes, madam, I wish my gratitude henceforth   1295
to incise your power in every heart; and now,
in anticipation, I bless this happy coldness
whose passing will renew the warmth of our love.
Whatever Pallas has done, enough, I forget it;
I reconcile myself with Britannicus;   1300
as for this love that caused our enmity,
I make you arbiter, you shall judge between us.
Go, then, and take this joyous word to my brother.
Guards! Let my mother's orders be obeyed.

                                        (*Exit Agrippina.*)

Burrus

My lord, this end of conflict, these embraces—   1305
what joy to see them! You know if in the past
my voice was ever contrary to her,
if I have ever wished to turn you against her,
and if I have merited this unjust rage.

Nero

To be quite truthful, I was displeased with you,   1310
 Burrus: I thought the two of you well agreed;

but her hostility gives you back my trust.
She is too hasty, Burrus, to think she has won.
I do embrace my rival, but to destroy him.

Burrus

What, sir!

Nero

            I have had too much: his death must free me,   1315
once for all, from her ravings. While he breathes
I only half live. She has worn me out
with the repetition of that hostile name.
Nor will I give her damned effrontery scope
to promise him my place a second time.   1320

Burrus

She will soon weep, then, for Britannicus?

Nero

Before the day ends I shall fear him no more.

Burrus

And what inspires you with this wish?

Nero

                          My honor,
my love, the safety of my days, my life.

Burrus

It is not so, my lord: this horrible plan,   1325
say what you will, was not conceived by you.

Nero

Burrus!

Burrus

      By heaven! I hear it from your mouth?
You yourself, without shuddering, could hear it?
Do you reflect what blood will be upon you?
Is Nero bored with the affection of men?   1330
What will they say? What do you think they will say?

Nero

So, chained to my past glory, I must keep
always before my eyes some dubious love
which chance, in one day, gives us and takes from us?
Subject to all their wishes, denying my own,   1335
am I their emperor solely to humor them?

Burrus
My lord, does it not satisfy your ambition
to see, among your works, the people's content?
It is for you to choose; you are still master.
Virtuous to this point, you can always be: 1340
the way is charted, nothing holds you back;
you have only to move on from good to good.
But if you follow the precepts of your flatterers
you will be driven, my lord, from crime to crime,
forced to defend one cruelty with another,   1345
and bathe your bloodied arms more deeply in blood.
Britannicus, dying, will stir up the zeal
of his friends, already eager to take his part.
And his avengers will find other champions,
who, even when dead, will have successors. You light   1350
an endless fire. Feared by the universe,
you must fear everyone: you must never fail
to punish, to be uneasy about your plans,
reckoning all your subjects as enemies.
Can the good fortune of your early life   1355
move you, my lord, to hate your innocence?
Do you recall the happiness of those years?
How tranquilly, O heaven, you saw them pass!
What pleasure to reflect, to tell yourself:
"At this time, everywhere, I am blessed, I am loved.   1360
The people do not start in fear at my name;
in all their weeping, heaven has never heard it;
their dark resentment does not turn from me
when I go by: their hearts are light about me
as if on wings." Such were your pleasures then.   1365
How changed, O Gods! You valued the poorest life.
One day the senate, I recall, quite justly,
urged you to sign the death of a guilty man;
you, sir, held out against their obdurate will:
your heart took it for cruelty; and repining   1370
at the grave trials of the emperorship,
"I wish," you said, "I had never learned to write."
No, either you believe me, or my death

will spare me from beholding this evil thing:
no one shall see that I outlive your honor,   1375
if you are bent upon such infamy.

(*Throwing himself at Nero's feet*)
                                    Here,
I am ready, sir: this heart, before you go,
must be run through, for it will not consent.
Summon the cruel men who have worked upon you;
let them come forth and try their unsteady hands.   1380
But now I see my grief touches my Emperor,
I see his virtue tremble before its rage.
Lose not a moment. Name the perjured men
who dare to breathe this counsel of parricide.
Call for your brother. Forget, embracing him—   1385

Nero

What do you ask of me?

Burrus

                        No, he does not hate you,
my lord; he has been falsely used; I know
his innocence; I answer for his obedience.
I go to urge this fond reunion at once.

Nero

Let him await me in my quarters, with you.   1390

(*Exit Burrus. Enter Narcissus.*)

Narcissus

Sir, I have all in hand for this righteous death,
the poison ready. For me, the famed Locusta
has spared no effort in her will to please:
she caused a slave to expire before my eyes.
To do it surely, the sword is not so quick   1395
as the new poison her hand confides to me.

Nero

Enough, Narcissus; I thank you for this care,
and do not wish you to go further.

Narcissus

                              What?
Your weakened hatred for Britannicus
forbids me—

Nero
Yes. We are being reconciled. 1400
Narcissus
I shall do nothing to dissuade you from this,
but today, sir, he has seen himself imprisoned:
this injury will long be fresh in his heart.
There are no secrets time does not reveal:
he'll know it was decided that by my hand 1405
he should receive a poison mixed at your order.
I pray the Gods divert him from that scheme,
but he will do, perhaps, what you dare not do.
Nero
I answer for his heart; I will conquer mine.
Narcissus
And Junia's marriage, sir, will bind your friendship? 1410
You make this sacrifice for him as well?
Nero
This is to care too much. Whatever comes,
I cease to count him among my enemies.
Narcissus
Sir, Agrippina had promised herself this;
she has regained her sovereign hold upon you. 1415
Nero
Why, then, what has she said? What do you mean?
Narcissus
She has been boasting of it quite publicly.
Nero
Of what?
Narcissus
That she need see you but a moment;
that all those outcries, all that ominous temper,
would be succeeded by a modest silence; 1420
that you would be the first to yield, content
that she should kindly deign to forget the past.
Nero
But, Narcissus, tell me, what would you have me do?
I am all too much inclined to punish her daring;
this reckless triumph, if I could have my way, 1425
would soon be followed by eternal regret.

109

But how will the world speak of it? Do you tell me
to launch myself upon the oppressor's course?
Shall Rome, effacing all those marks of honor,
leave me, in place of all, the name of poisoner? 1430
They'll look upon my vengeance as parricide.

Narcissus

And are you governed, sir, by their caprice?
Did you expect them to keep still forever?
Is it for you to listen to them? Do you
forget your own desires? Will you yourself 1435
be the one person to whom you do not dare
give credence? But, sir, you do not know the Romans.
No, no, they are more restrained in their spoken thoughts.
So much precaution weakens your government;
they will believe, in fact, they deserve your fear. 1440
They are long reconciled to the yoke. They adore
the hand that keeps them tethered: you will see them
forever burning to gratify your wishes.
Their avid slavery wore Tiberious out.
I myself, exercising a borrowed power 1445
which I received from Claudius with my freedom,
a hundred times in my past years of glory
have tried their patience without tiring it.
You fear the stigma of a poisoning? Rule
that the brother perish, cast the sister off, 1450
and Rome, heaping the victims on its altars,
though they were innocent, will discover their crimes;
you will see ranked among the unlucky days
those when the sister and the brother were born.

Nero

Once more, Narcissus, I cannot undertake it. 1455
I have promised Burrus. I was forced to yield.
I do not wish again, by breaking my word,
to give his virtue arms against me. I set
my courage uselessly against his reasoning;
I do not hear him with a tranquil heart. 1460

Narcissus

Burrus does not believe all that he says:
his adroit virtue looks to his interest, sir;

or rather, all of them have a single thought:
by this stroke they would see their power thrust down;
you would be free, then, sir, and those proud masters   1465
would bend their will to yours as we others do.
Do you know nothing of what they dare to say?
"Nero"—to hear them tell it—"was not born
to the emperorship; he speaks and acts by rule.
His heart is Burrus. His mind is Seneca.   1470
For all ambition, for distinctive virtue,
he excels at racing chariots, eager to win
prizes unworthy of his hands; he is pleased
to make himself a spectacle for the Romans,
to let his voice pour forth upon a theater   1475
in songs he'd have them think divine—while, moving
now and again among them, his soldiers try
to extract for him the grudging plaudits." Ah!
will you not force them to be silent?
Nero

                            Come,
Narcissus. We shall see what we must do.   1480

III

ACT FIVE

(Enter Britannicus and Junia.)

Britannicus

    Yes, madam, Nero (who had looked for this?)
    is waiting in his private rooms to embrace me.
    He is inviting there the youth of the court;
    he'd have the pomp and jubilance of a banquet
    impress them with the good faith of our vows   1485
    and warm our greetings. He stifles in himself
    that love, the source of so much hate; he gives you
    the full choice of my destiny. As for me,
    though banished from the rank of my ancestors,
    though he takes, before my eyes, what they have left me,   1490
    since now, no longer hostile to my love,
    he seems to yield me the glory of winning you,
    my heart, I will confess, in secret forgives,
    and with more resignation leaves him the rest.
    What! I am kept no longer apart from you?   1495
    Even at this moment I may look untroubled
    into those eyes which neither longing nor threats
    have moved, which have sacrificed for me the empire,
    the Emperor? Ah, my lady! . . . But what new fear,
    in the presence of my joy, constrains your own?   1500
    Why, as I see you listening, do your eyes,
    your sad eyes, turn with long regards toward heaven?
    What do you fear?

Junia

             I myself do not know,
    and yet I fear.

Britannicus

          You love me?

Junia

               Alas, indeed!

Britannicus
  Nero no longer troubles our happiness.   1505
Junia
  But do you answer for his sincerity?
Britannicus
  What? You suspect him of a stealthy hate?
Junia
  A moment past he loved me. He swore your death.
  Now he avoids me, seeking you: my lord,
  can one brief moment work so great a change?   1510
Britannicus
  This, madam, is Agrippina's work. She thought
  my condemnation was bringing with it her own.
  Thanks to the foresight of her jealous spirit,
  our greatest enemies have taken our part.
  I trust the excitement she has shown me; I trust   1515
  in Burrus; even his master, I believe,
  at my example, incapable of treachery,
  hates open-heartedly or ceases to hate.
Junia
  Sir, do not judge his heart by yours; your ways
  run contrary. I have had but one day's knowledge   1520
  of Nero and the court, but in this court—
  if I may dare the observation—alas,
  how far is all one says from what one thinks,
  how little are the mind and heart agreed,
  with what enjoyment, here, is a promise broken!   1525
  A curious resting-place for you, for me!
Britannicus
  But whether a true friend or false, if Nero
  still troubles you, is he himself untroubled?
  No, no, he'll not provoke, by a cowardly crime,
  the people and the senate to rise against him.   1530
  But, more than this, he knows his late injustice.
  His deep regret, even to Narcissus, was plain.
  If he had told you, my Princess, to what point—
Junia
  But, sir, is not Narcissus betraying you?

Britannicus
Why would you have me doubt him?
Junia
                    Can I know?   1535
Your life is threatened. I am suspicious of all:
I fear they are all corrupted. I fear Nero;
I fear the bad luck that attends me. Warned
by a dark presentiment despite myself,
I am unwilling that you should leave my sight.   1540
Alas, if this agreement you count upon
were covering some device against your person!
If Nero, angered by our mutual pledge,
had chosen the night to mask his vengeance: if now,
while I am with you, he were setting his snares,   1545
if I were speaking to you for the last time!
Ah, Prince!
Britannicus
             But you are weeping. My dear Princess!
And your heart is concerned for me so much?
Can this be? On a day when, in his pride,
Nero expects to dazzle you, in this place   1550
where all avoid me and honor him, to prefer
my misery to the splendors of his court?
What? On this same day, in these same surroundings,
to scorn an empire and to weep for me?
But, madam, calm those precious tears; your doubts   1555
will quickly be dispelled by my return.
To delay longer would invite suspicion.
Adieu. I am going, heart filled with my love,
amid the revelry of those blind youths,
aware of nothing but my shining Princess.   1560
Adieu.
Junia
     Prince—
Britannicus
           They expect me. I must go.
Junia
But wait at least till you are summoned.

(Enter Agrippina.)

Agrippina
                    Prince,
what has delayed you? Go with all dispatch:
Nero is restless, carping at your absence.
The mirth and pleasure of the company wait   1565
the signal of your greetings to sparkle forth.
Do not permit that honest wish to droop.
Go. And now, madam, let us join Octavia.
Britannicus
Go, lovely Junia, and with a happy mind
hasten to greet my sister, who awaits you.   1570
          (To Agrippina)
I will come to you directly when I am free,
to thank you, madam, for your good offices.
                              (Exit Britannicus.)
Agrippina
I am deceived or there were tears in your eyes
at his leave-taking, madam. May I know
what trouble formed this cloud? Do you mistrust   1575
a peace I am concerned to make secure?
Junia
After the many trials this day has cost me,
how could I reassure my frantic spirits?
As yet I have hardly grasped this miracle.
If I should fear some threat to your good deeds,   1580
change, madam, is a frequent thing at court,
and some fear is inseparable from love.
Agrippina
Enough. I have spoken: all is quite reversed.
I have left no room for your suspicions. I vouch
for an agreement sworn between my hands: 1585
the pledges Nero gave me are too convincing.
If you had seen with what affection he proved
the new sincerity of his promises,
with what embraces, only now, he detained me!!
When I took leave he would not let me go;   1590
his frank good humor written upon his face,
he deigned to tell me of small intimate things

at first, like any son discoursing freely
in his mother's presence, putting off his pride.
But soon, with a stern countenance again,   1595
as of an emperor who consults his mother,
his august confidence placed in my hands
secrets that touch the destiny of men.
No, I must here confess it to his glory:
there is no guilty malice in his heart;   1600
only our enemies, perverting his goodness,
made use of his obliging nature against us.
But in the end their power declines; once more
Rome will know Agrippina: already it hears,
adoringly, of my return to grace.   1605
Come, let us not wait here for night, but go
to join Octavia, giving her what's left
of a day as happy as I believed it cursed.
But what is this I hear? What confused tumult?

Junia

O heaven! Save Britannicus!

(Enter Burrus.)

Agrippina

                      Where now   1610
so quickly, Burrus? Stop. What is the meaning—

Burrus

It is over, madam. Britannicus expires.

Junia

   My prince!

Agrippina

          He is dying?

Burrus

                  Or more truly, madam,
he is dead.

Junia

         Madam, forgive this frenzy. I go
to help him, if I can, or to follow him.   1615

(Exit Junia.)

Agrippina

Burrus, what a foul deed!

Burrus
>   I cannot survive it.
  I must leave the court, the Emperor.
Agrippina
>   Is it true?
  He has had no horror of his brother's blood?
Burrus
  This plot has been more subtly carried out.
  The Emperor, seeing his brother there, directly   1620
  rose and embraced him. All were silent. At once
  Caesar, beginning, took a cup in his hand:
"To end this day under better auspices,
  my hand pours out the first drops of this wine,"
  he said; "Gods, whom I call to this libation,   1625
  come, prosper our reunion." Britannicus
  in the same manner made his pledge, the cup,
  as he held it, being replenished by Narcissus.
  But when his lips had scarcely touched its brim
  the effect was seen, more puissant than the sword: 1630
  madam, the shining look was snatched from his eyes.
  He fell upon his couch—cold, lifeless. Judge
  how startling the impression on every soul:
  half the guests, in a frightened uproar, withdrew;
  but those with more experience of the court,   1635
  watching the eyes of Caesar, composed their faces.
  Meanwhile upon his couch he remained at ease,
  untouched, it seemed, by all the astonishment.
"This malady," he said, "whose rudeness you fear
  has often, without peril, attacked his childhood."   1640
  Narcissus tried in vain to affect concern;
  his cunning joy, despite himself, glared out.
  For my part, though the Emperor punish my boldness,
  I struggled through the press of an odious court,
  and was going away, heartbroken by this murder,   1645
  to mourn Britannicus, Caesar, the whole State.
Agrippina
  He is coming. You will see if I inspired him.

JEAN RACINE

(Enter Nero and Narcissus.)

Nero
  Gods!
Agrippina
        Nero, a word with you. Britannicus
  is dead. I recognize by what device;
  I know the assassin.
Nero
                    Who is it, madam?
Agrippina
                            You.   1650
Nero
  I? Now we see how far your suspicions go.
  There is no evil for which I am not to blame:
  and if one listens to you, it was my hand,
  no doubt, that finished Claudius too. His son
  was dear to you: his death may cloud your reason.   1655
  I cannot answer for the blows of fate.
Agrippina
  No, no, Britannicus was poisoned: Narcissus
  saw to the execution. You ordered it.
Nero
  Madam! . . . But who tells you such things?
Narcissus
                            Ah, well,
  is this suspicion so outrageous, my lord?   1660
  Britannicus, madam, had some secret plans
  that would have cost you some more apt regrets.
  He aspired to greater things than marrying Junia:
  he would have punished you for your own well-doing.
  He tricked even you; and his offended heart   1665
  sought, now or later, to revive the past.
  Then, whether fate has served you against your will,
  or whether, knowing the plots that threatened him,
  Caesar trusted himself to my loyalty,
  leave the tears to your enemies. Let them count   1670
  this ill chance with the most unlucky; but you. . . .

Agrippina
  Continue, Nero, with such ministers.
  You will be known for glorious deeds. Continue.
  You did not take this step that you might turn back.
  Your hand commences with your brother's blood;   1675
  I can see it reach even to your mother. I know
  you hate me in your deepest heart; you will wish
  to free yourself from the yoke of my benefits.
  But even my death I would make useless to you.
  Do not suppose I shall leave you tranquil. Rome,   1680
  this sky, this light of day you received from me,
  each moment, everywhere, will bring me before you.
  Regrets will come like furies, which you will try
  to calm with new barbarities; your madness,
  aggravating itself as it runs its course,   1685
  will mark each day with still more novel blood.
  But heaven, I trust, weary at last of your crimes,
  will add you to so many other victims.
  I trust, with their blood and with mine upon you,
  you will be given no choice but to shed your own;   1690
  and in the times to come, your name will appear
  to the most cruel tyrants a cruel insult.
  This is the end my heart presages for you.
  Goodbye, you may leave.
Nero

                 Narcissus, come with me.
                    (*Exeunt Nero and Narcissus.*)
Agrippina
  Ah, heaven! How baseless my suspicions were: 1695
  I condemned Burrus, to listen to Narcissus!
  Did you see, Burrus, when Nero took his leave,
  what furious looks he gave me? It is over;
  he has nothing more to stop him. Now the blow
  predicted to me will fall upon my head.   1700
  He will crush you in your turn, as well.
Burrus

                    Ah, madam,
  as for myself, I have lived one day too long.

I would to heaven that, fortunately cruel,
he had made me the first victim of his madness,
and had not given me, in this somber crime,   1705
too certain proof of the State's evil plight.
His crime itself is not my whole despair;
his jealousy might urge his brother's death;
to explain my grief, madam, it was that Nero
saw him die without changing color. His eyes   1710
already have the impassive constancy
of a tyrant hardened in foul play since childhood.
Let him finish. Let him purge a minister
who annoys him, one who cannot bear that sight.
No, far from wishing to avoid his anger,   1715
the earliest death will be most grateful to me.

                                      (*Enter Albina.*)

Albina

Ah, madam! sir! Come quickly to the Emperor.
Come, defend Caesar from his own stricken mind.
He sees himself eternally separated
from Junia.

Agrippina

                 What! Junia has ended her life?   1720

Albina

To make his grief eternal, without dying,
my lady, she is dead for him. You know
how impulsively she darted from these rooms.
She pretended to be going to sad Octavia;
but soon she turned and took a different course,   1725
through which I have kept her running steps in sight.
Having gone wildly through the palace gates,
she saw, at once, the statue of Augustus,
and, moistening with her tears its marble feet,
while in her arms she held it tightly clasped,   1730
"Prince, by these knees which I embrace," she said,
"protect, today, the last of your progeny.
Rome, in your house, has just seen sacrificed
your one descendant who could compare with you.
I am ordered to betray him after his death;   1735
but to keep pure my covenant with him,

I pledge myself to those immortal Gods
whose altars, by your virtue's grace, you share."
The people, meanwhile, whom this sight astonished,
ran from all sides, pressed round, were moved to pity   1740
by her great sorrow, and with a single voice
agreed to take her under their guardianship.
They led her to the temple, where through the years
our virgins destined for the altars' cult
guard faithfully the precious store of fire   1745
kept burning for our Gods. Nero came out
to watch them leave, but dared not call them back.
Narcissus, bolder, quick to please him, sped
toward Junia undeterred, with profane hand
thrust out to stop her. His audacity   1750
was punished by a thousand mortal blows;
his faithless blood came spattering upon Junia.
Caesar, amazed by all these things at once,
left him among the hands that closed him round,
and sought the palace. Everyone avoids   1755
his brutal silence: only Junia's name
escapes his mouth. In search of nothing, he roams;
his eyes dare not lift up their haggard glances;
and when the night comes, joining with solitude
to embitter the mute rage of his despair,   1760
if you should leave him longer uncomforted,
his grief might soon take arms against his life.
Time presses: go to him. By a mere caprice
he would destroy himself.

Agrippina

                              He would do justly.
But, Burrus, let us see to what intent   1765
these passions work, what change remorse may bring,
and if, henceforth, he would follow other precepts.

Burrus

Would to the Gods this crime might be his last!

121

PHAEDRA

Let's fly into the night of hell. This is the terrible cry of Phaedra; and while human desire attaches itself to the forbidden or forbidding object, there will be those who understand the cry. *Phèdre* is no doubt the most powerful study of a sexual obsession ever written for the theater, but it has always been recognized as something more. After the fashion of masterpieces, it offers somewhat different truths to different times. Almost every generation has found new reasons to admire it.

Today, of course, we think that we understand its full greatness and orginality; as A. F. B. Clark says in his astute *Jean Racine,* we can see how perfectly it fuses the Greek sense of fatality with the Christian sense of grace withheld, and how it seems to foreshadow some of the reigning insights of modern psychology. Even if it were not regarded as Racine's greatest play, it would have a special interest for us; it is concerned with the sense of guilt, which is thought to be our most frequent substitute for the conviction of sin. Here the emotion of guilt exists in an unqualified and unendurable form. It is the result of no action whatever, but rather demands and induces an action that will be outrageous enough to justify it.

There is scarcely a hint of this theme in Racine's two literary sources, the *Hippolytus* of Euripides and the *Phaedra* of Seneca. Two important scenes, in their general outline, were taken from each play, but the verbal homology is almost unrelated to the dramatic effect. It is curious to see how Racine makes use of various elements of the original plot by shaping them to his own purpose; even the letter, in Euripides a murder-ous and decisive act, the turning point of the play, is retained as a small incident, disposed of in two lines, to illustrate the tortured irresolution of Racine's Phaedra. Often the characters themselves, in order to strength-en sympathy for the heroine, are made to give quite a different impres-sion while speaking almost the same words. It was both daring and in-genious, for example, to show the great Theseus as a blustering hypocrite, and afterward, by imperceptible degrees, to lift him to the dignified pathos which he assumes in the end.

Racine cannot give us, indeed he does not attempt, either the mystical grandeur or the touching realism of Euripides: the impassioned choric songs and the racy old wives' talk of the nurse are equally beyond his range. Nevertheless, his feeling for the Greek play and its legendary background found expression in a certain haunting quality—an effect of incantation that far transcends, though it does not impair, the virtues of clarity and concinnity which his age admired. He himself noted it, possibly with surprise, when he spoke in his preface of the charm of myth, "which contributes enormously to poetry." Here his characteristic style, at once sculptured and flowing, very often rises to the lyricism from which it has usually seemed careful to refrain.

We can be sure that to Racine and his contemporaries the story had a religious bearing. In this play the Gods are as important as the char-acters; their presence is as real, their silence articulate. Phaedra's struggle is seen to be hopeless because it is not merely against herself but against a divine force. Such an argument goes directly to the question of free will: it was a survival of Racine's early Jansenist training, and it would have been intolerable to religious orthodoxy if it had not been stated in terms of Greek myth. The implications were clear. This was the plight of every human being who, believing in a freedom of choice that makes him accountable, nevertheless feels himself to be irresistibly impelled.

Such an emphasis on fate, joined with the idea of individual respon-sibility, was in line with the contemporary predestinarian philosophy; it was one of the paradoxes that appealed to the intellectualism of the time, attracting some of the greatest minds to Jansenism—"the difficult faith"—before it was suppressed. Racine made it come to life, in this reunion of the self-martyrizing conscience and the ancient *fatum*. It is what associates him with Pascal and even, faintly, with Hobbes; it is what separates him from the Platonists and from the stoic individualism of Corneille. Mauriac states it with justice when he says that Phaedra's ruling divinity is "not a blind fate, but on the contrary one that is terribly attentive to the ruin of souls condemned before their birth."

This most celebrated of women's roles was first played by La Champmeslé, the great actress of the time, who was then in her middle thirties. Racine had loved her for years—unhappily, for she was surrounded by rich and noble admirers. She had made her reputation in his plays, beginning with the role of Hermione in a 1670 production of *Andromaque;* since then, all her parts had been written for her. She was very famous. Nevertheless the opening of *Phèdre,* on January 1, 1677, was as much a fiasco as that of *Britannicus,* and for a more invidious reason. A group of Racine's enemies, financed by the Duchesse de Bouillon, were backing another *Phèdre,* by Pradon, which was to open in two days at the Guénégaud. At the cost of 15,000 pounds they had bought up all the desirable tickets for the first six performances at both theaters, so that the Bourgogne was deserted while Pradon's play opened to a full house. On the strength of this pseudo-triumph it ran for five months, and that was the end of it. The plot turned to Racine's advantage by making the originality of his play even more striking, as the *Mercure Galant* noted at the time. But this experience and the bitter events that followed it, culminating in a final tempestuous break with La Champmeslé, undoubtedly helped to bring on the subjective crisis which caused him, in this year, to abandon the theater, to accept an appointment as royal historiographer, and to become a devoted husband and father for the rest of his life.

He had lived thirty-seven of his fifty-nine years, fourteen in the theater, and had written ten plays. *Phèdre* was the ninth and last of his so-called profane tragedies. Twelve years later he finished *Esther,* and after another two years, *Athalie,* both written at the request of the first lady of the court, Madame de Maintenon, who had wanted something appropriate for the young elocutionists at Saint-Cyr, a royally sponsored girls' school. These two great biblical tragedies, in which he used choric passages for the first time, contain his most majestic poetry. They were never given publicly while he lived. In this last decade he wrote also some of the most flawless lyric poems in French, the four *Cantiques Spirituels.*

CHARACTERS

Theseus
King of Athens and son of Aegeus

Phaedra
Wife of Theseus, daughter of Minos and Pasiphaë

Hippolytus
Son of Theseus and Antiope, queen of the Amazons

Aricia
Princess of the blood royal of Athens

Theramenes
Tutor of Hippolytus

Oenone
Nurse and confidante of Phaedra

Ismene
Confidante of Aricia

Panope
A woman of Phaedra's suite

Guards

The scene is laid in Troezen, a city of the Peloponnesus

ACT ONE

(*Enter Hippolytus and Theramenes.*)

Hippolytus

Resolved: I am leaving, dear Theramenes.
My sojourn in delightful Troezen is ended.
In this anxiety, this mortal doubt,
I begin to be ashamed of my idleness.
More than six months away from my father, I know   5
nothing of what befalls so dear a life,
nor even in what place he may be hidden.

Theramenes

Where, then, sir, will you look for him? Already,
to satisfy your reasonable fear,
I have crossed the two seas Corinth separates,   10
inquired for Theseus among the tribes of that shore
where the Acheron flows down to the dead; I have searched
Elis, and, passing Taenarus, have gone
as far as the sea where Icarus fell. On the strength
of what new hope, under what fortunate skies,   15
do you expect to find his trace? Indeed,
who fathoms, who can say, if the King your father
wishes the mystery of his absence known,
or if, while we tremble for his life, that hero
may not be hiding a new love affair,   20
quietly waiting till some deluded woman—

Hippolytus

Stop, dear Theramenes. Respect Theseus.
Now and in future free from his young errors,
he is not held by a base obstacle.
Phaedra, checking the fatal restlessness   25
of his desires, long since has feared no rival.
In seeking him I shall follow my duty, at last,
and leave this country I dare no longer see.

127

Theramenes

Ah? And since when, my lord, do you fear the sight
of this peaceful country you have loved since childhood,   30
which I have always known you to prefer
to the pompous tumult of Athens and the court?
What danger—rather, what grief drives you away?

Hippolytus

That time is past. All wears a different face,
all's changed, since to these shores the Gods have sent   35
the daughter of Minos and Pasiphaë.

Theramenes

I understand: I know the cause of your suffering.
The presence of Phaedra hurts you, offends your sight.
Dangerous stepmother, she had scarcely seen you
when at once your exile furnished proof of her power.   40
But her old rancor, centering in the past
on you, either has vanished or much abated.
Besides, what danger have you cause to fear
from a dying woman, one who seeks to die?
Stricken with an ill she will not disclose,   45
weary, indeed, of herself and the light of day,
can Phaedra design anything against you?

Hippolytus

Her vain spite does not move me. Hippolytus,
in leaving, avoids another enemy:
I avoid, I will confess it, that young Aricia,   50
last of a fatal blood sworn to our doom.

Theramenes

What? Even you, my lord, would punish her?
When did the gracious sister of Pallas' sons
join in the plots of her disloyal brothers?
And must you hate her innocent loveliness?   55

Hippolytus

If I hated her I would not fly from her.

Theramenes

Sir, may I venture to explain your flight?
Are you no longer that proud Hippolytus,
implacably defying the amorous law,
the yoke Theseus so many times has borne?   60

Can Venus, having been so long despised,
Intend to justify your father at last,
and, putting you on a level with other men,
force you to carry incense to her altars?
Are you in love, sir?   65

Hippolytus

            Dare you say it, friend?
You who have known my heart since I drew breath,
can you expect me to deny in shame
its proud and scornful sentiments? Not only
was I nourished at the breast of an Amazon
upon this pride you think astonishing;   70
grown to a riper age, I understood
my own good fortune when I knew myself.
You, closely bound to me by a true zeal,
would tell me, then, the history of my father.
You know how, hanging upon your words, my spirit   75
took fire from the recital of his great deeds,
when you would bring to mind that intrepid hero
consoling mortals for Alcides' loss:
that tale of monsters choked and brigands punished,
Procrustes, Sinis, Sciron, Cercyon,   80
the Epidaurian giant, his scattered bones,
Crete sultry with the blood of the Minotaur.
But when you told me the less glorious part,
his pledge on all sides given and believed—
Helen abducted from her home in Sparta,   85
and then, in Salamis, Periboea's tears;
so many more, whose names he has forgotten,
too trusting souls his passion has beguiled:
Ariadne crying to the rocks, and Phaedra
borne off, at last, under a better omen—   90
you know how, listening against my will,
I often begged you to cut short the tale,
glad if I might have stripped from memory
that sorry half of an account so splendid.
Would I, then, in my turn, accept those bonds?   95
Would the Gods have humbled me so much? Even more
contemptible, in my unmanly sighing,

since a long roll of honors pleads for Theseus,
while yet no monsters by my hands subdued
have given me the right to falter so.   100
But even if my pride were reconciled,
would I have chosen Aricia to conquer me?
Would my ungoverned senses not recall
the eternal obstacle between us? My father
rejects her: by a stern law he decrees   105
no nephew shall be given to her brothers.
Fearing the offshoot of a guilty stock,
he would have their name die with their sister: for her,
submitted to his guardianship till death,
never the fires of Hymen shall be lighted.   110
Should I defend her rights against his anger?
Shall I give precedent to temerity,
launching my youth in a foolhardy love—

Theramenes

Ah, if your hour has once been marked, my lord,
heaven will little care for our arguments.   115
Theseus opens your eyes, wishing to close them;
his hatred, fanning a rebellious flame,
imparts a new grace to his enemy.
Indeed, why be afraid of a virtuous love?
If it have some sweetness, dare you not essay it?   120
Though you may have some thorny scruple still,
can one go astray in the steps of Hercules?
What wilful hearts has Venus not subdued?
Where would you be, even you who strive against her,
if, though opposing her, Antiope   125
had not burned with a chaste desire for Theseus?
But of what use to parry with fine words?
Confess it, all must change; and for some time
you have been seen less often, proud and shy,
speeding a chariot along the shore,   130
or, master of the art revealed by Neptune,
breaking an untamed courser to the bit.
The forest sounds less often with our cries;
charged with a secret flame, your eyes grow heavy.
No doubt of it: you love, you are consumed,   135

you perish of an ill you attempt to hide.
Has the delightful Aricia found your heart?
Hippolytus
Theramenes, I go in search of my father.
Theramenes
Will you not see Phaedra, sir, before you leave?
Hippolytus
It is my intention: you may tell her so.   140
Let us see her, since my duty orders it.
But what new grief troubles her dear Oenone?
                              (*Enter Oenone.*)
Oenone
Alas! What trouble, sir, can equal mine?
The Queen's near to her fatal hour. I keep
my watch upon her night and day, in vain: 145
she dies in my arms of an unspoken ill.
A long confusion reigns within her mind.
Her restless torment drags her from her bed:
she would see the morning light, yet her deep sorrow
commands me to keep everyone away—   150
she is coming.
Hippolytus
                  It is enough: I leave her here,
and do not show her a detested face.
            (*Exeunt Hippolytus and Theramenes. Enter Phaedra.*)
Phaedra
No farther, dear Oenone. Let us stop here.
I can stand up no longer: strength deserts me.
My eyes are dazzled to see the light again,   155
and my knees tremble and give way beneath me.
Alas!
                              (*She sits down.*)
Oenone
            Almighty Gods, may our tears quiet you!
Phaedra
How these vain ornaments and veils oppress me!
What meddling fingers, tying all these knots,
have troubled to bind up my hair on my brow?   160
All things afflict and hurt me, conspire to hurt me.

Oenone

How all her wishes quarrel, one with another!
Just now, repenting of your wicked plan,
you set our fingers flying to deck you out;
as though recalling your old energy,   165
you wished to show yourself, to see the day.
You see it, madam; and now, ready to hide,
you hate the brightness you have come to seek?

Phaedra

Noble and brilliant author of a sad race,
you whom my mother proudly claimed for sire,   170
you, red with shame, perhaps, for my wretchedness,
Sun, I have come to see you for the last time.

Oenone

What? Will you not give up that cruel wish?
Am I to see you always renouncing life,
making these mournful preparations?   175

Phaedra

                         Gods!

To be sitting now in the shadow of the forest!
When will my eyes again, through the noble dust,
follow a chariot flying in its course?

Oenone

What, madam?

Phaedra

                Senseless—where am I? What have I said?
Where have my purpose and my reason wandered?   180
They are lost: the Gods have spoiled me of their use.
Oenone, the blood burns upon my face:
I let you see too much my shameful sorrows.
My eyes, against my will, are full of tears.

Oenone

Ah, if you have to blush, blush for a silence   185
that aggravates the bitterness of your pain.
Resisting all our cares, deaf to our words,
would you, so cold and heartless, end your days?
What madness cuts them off half spent? What charm
or subtle mischief has dried up their source?   190

Three times the darkness has obscured the sky
since sleep has touched your eyelids, and three times
the rising sun has driven away the night
while you have languished without nourishment.
By what affraying purpose are you tempted?   195
By what right do you seek to kill yourself?
You offend the Gods, the authors of your life,
betray the husband to whom your vow is sworn.
You do indeed betray your unhappy children,
thrusting them early under a hard yoke.   200
Think: the same day that robs them of their mother
will give back confidence to the stranger's son,
proud enemy of yours, of all your race,
that son an Amazon carried in her womb,
Hippolytus—

Phaedra

        Ah, Gods!

Oenone

                That touches you.   205

Phaedra

Wretched, what name has fallen from your mouth?

Oenone

Well, now, your anger flares with cause. I like
to see you shudder at that fatal name.
Live, then. Let love, let duty urge you to it.
Live: let it not befall that a Scythian's son,   210
crushing your children under hateful laws,
should rule the fairest blood of Greece and the Gods.
But now delay no more. Each moment kills you.
Repair at once your all but ruined strength,
while your life keeps, though burning low and poor,   215
some little ember that may be revived.

Phaedra

I have too much prolonged its guilty term.

Oenone

What? Are you torn apart by some remorse?
What crime could weigh so constantly upon you?
Your hands have not been stained with innocent blood?   220

Phaedra

My hands, thank heaven, are not criminal.
Would to the Gods my heart were as innocent!

Oenone

Then what atrocious plan have you conceived,
that it strikes terror to your heart even now?

Phaedra

I have told enough. Let me be spared the rest.   225
I die, that the fatal thing be undiscovered.

Oenone

Die, then. Hold fast to an inhuman silence;
but look for another hand to close your eyes.
While there remains to you a feeble spark,
my soul among the dead shall first descend.   230
A thousand open roads lead there forever,
and my just grief will choose the most direct.
When, cruel one, has my devotion failed you?
When you were born, did not my arms receive you?
My home, my children, I left all for you.   235
Thus true, was I to be rewarded thus?

Phaedra

What fruit do you expect from so much forcing?
You will shake with horror if I break the silence.

Oenone

What will you tell me that can match the horror
of seeing you destroyed before my eyes?   240

Phaedra

When you know my crime, the fate that overcomes me,
I shall die none the less for it, but guiltier.

Oenone

My lady, by these tears I have shed for you,
by your poor faltering knees which I embrace,
release my spirit from this mortal doubt.   245

Phaedra

You will have it. Rise.

Oenone

           Speak. I am listening.

Phaedra

                                        Gods!
What shall I say to her? And where begin?
Oenone
Now punish me no more with vain alarms.
Phaedra
O enmity of Venus! Fatal anger!
Into what errors love impelled my mother!   250
Oenone
Let us forget them, madam; for all the future,
may a long silence cover this memory.
Phaedra
Ariadne, my sister, of what wounded love
you died abandoned on the seashore!
Oenone
                                        Madam,
what are you saying? What mortal bitterness   255
incites you against all your race today?
Phaedra
Since Venus wishes it, of that doomed race
I die the last and the most miserable.
Oenone
Are you in love?
Phaedra
                        I have love's total fury.
Oenone
For whom?
Phaedra
                        Now you will hear the peak of horrors.   260
I love—at that fatal name, I am cold, I quake—
I love—
Oenone
            Whom?
Phaedra
                        You know that son of the Amazon,
that prince so long, now, by myself oppressed?
Oenone
Hippolytus? Great Gods!

Phaedra

It was you that named him.

Oenone

Just heaven! My blood runs cold in every vein.   265
O hopelessness! O crime! Deplorable race!
Ill-fated journey! O unlucky coast,
why need we have come near your dangerous shore?

Phaedra

My ill goes further back. When newly bound
under the marriage law to Aegeus' son,   270
when my repose, my happiness seemed sure,
Athens revealed my superb enemy.
I saw him. I blushed, I went pale at his sight;
my soul was troubled and undone; my eyes
could see no longer, nor my lips speak; I felt   275
my body turn to flame, yet shook with cold.
I knew that it was Venus, her dreadful fires,
the certain torment of the blood she pursues.
By constant vows I hoped to turn them aside;
I built her a temple, garnished it with care.   280
Surrounded by the victims night and day,
I looked into their bodies for my lost reason.
Poor remedies for an incurable love!
In vain upon the altars I burned incense:
when my lips cried to the Goddess, I adored   285
Hippolytus. Seeing him constantly,
even before those altars I kept burning,
I offered all to that god I dared not name.
I fled him everywhere. O final misery,
to rediscover him in his father's face!   290
Against myself, at last, I dared to rebel:
I whipped my courage up to persecute him.
To banish the enemy whom I idolized
I feigned the humors of a harsh stepmother.
Urging his exile, my continual plaints   295
wrested him from his father's arms and care.
I breathed again, Oenone; with his absence,
my life, less troubled, ran an innocent course.
Obedient to my husband, hiding my pain,

I nursed the fruits of his unlucky marriage.   300
Worthless precautions! Savage destiny!
Here, by my lord himself to Troezen led,
I saw the enemy I had sent afar,
and my too living wound began to bleed.
No more an ardor in my veins concealed,   305
it is Venus, wholly fastened upon her prey.
I have conceived for my crime a righteous fear;
hating my life, in horror of my love,
I wished by dying to protect my name
and hide from view a longing so infamous: 310
but I could not endure your tears, your strife;
I have told you all and I will not repent
if, in respect for my approaching death,
you burden me no more with unjust plaints,
and cease from your vain efforts to revive   315
a little warmth now all but breathed away.

                                        (Enter Panope.)

Panope
Would I could keep obscured from you sad news,
my lady, but I am bound to tell you. Death
has taken from you your invincible husband.
All know of this calamity but you.   320
Oenone
Panope, what are you saying?
Panope
                      That the trustful Queen
vainly implores of heaven the return of Theseus.
From ships reaching the port, Hippolytus,
his son, has but now learned his death.
Phaedra
                        Ah, heaven!
Panope
In the choice of master, Athens is divided.   325
Some have declared, madam, for the Prince your son.
Others, forgetting the state laws, make bold
to give the foreigner's son their loyalty.
An insolent cabal, it is even said,
would enthrone Aricia and the blood of Pallas.   330

I thought I must inform you of this danger.
Hippolytus intends to leave at once,
and, it is feared, arriving in this new storm,
may carry with him a whole inconstant people.

Oenone

Panope, it is enough. The Queen, who hears you,   335
by no means will neglect this serious warning.

                                       (*Exit Panope.*)

My lady, I had ceased urging you to live.
I had resolved to follow you to the tomb,
nor had more words or breath to turn you from it.
But this new grief imposes other laws.   340
Your fortune changes, wears another face.
Madam, the King is dead. You must succeed him.
He leaves a son to whom you owe yourself—
a slave if you are lost, a king if you live.
On whom, in his misfortune, can he lean?   345
No hand will move to wipe away his tears;
his blameless cries will carry to the Gods,
to rouse his ancestors against his mother.
Live. You need no longer reproach yourself.
Your love becomes an ordinary love.   350
In dying, Theseus has dissolved the ties
that were all the crime and horror of your longing.
Hippolytus is less forbidding to you,
and you can see him without burden of guilt.
Perhaps, convinced of your hostility,   355
he plans to become leader of the sedition.
Now undeceive his error, bend his will.
King of this happy coast, his share is Troezen,
but he knows well that the law gives your son
those superb ramparts which Minerva built.   360
Both of you have a natural enemy:
then stand united, to oppose Aricia.

Phaedra

Ah, well, let it be so! I yield to your counsel.
Let us live, if I can be brought back to life—
if, in this dark hour, fondness for a son   365
can touch my spirit and revive what's left.

ACT TWO

(Enter Aricia and Ismene.)

Aricia

    He asks to see me here? Hippolytus
    has sent to find me and would say goodbye?
    Ismene, this is the truth? You are not mistaken?

Ismene

    It is the first effect of Theseus' death.   370
    Prepare, madam, to see from every side
    the hearts estranged by Theseus flying toward you.
    Aricia, in the end, commands her fate,
    and soon all Greece will bow to her in homage.

Aricia

    Then it is not an idle rumor, Ismene?   375
    No longer a slave? I have no enemy?

Ismene

    Madam, the Gods no longer are averse.
    The shade of Theseus has rejoined your brothers.

Aricia

    What happened, do they say, to end his days?

Ismene

    They tell incredible stories of his death.   380
    Some say that, while abducting a new mistress,
    that false husband was swallowed by the sea.
    Some even say—this tale runs everywhere—
    he descended with Pirithous into Hades,
    saw the dark banks of the Cocytus, showed   385
    himself alive to the infernal shades,
    but could not leave that gloomy resting-place
    and pass the brink that no one crosses twice.

Aricia

    Shall I believe a mortal, before his hour,
    can penetrate the deep home of the dead?   390
    What charm could lure him to those fearful shores?

Ismene

He is dead, my lady; you alone still doubt.
Athens laments it. Troezen, being informed,
recognizes Hippolytus as king.
Within this palace, trembling for her son,   395
Phaedra takes counsel with her troubled friends.

Aricia

And you believe, more human than his father,
Hippolytus will give me lighter bonds,
will pity my misfortunes?

Ismene

      I believe it.

Aricia

The insensible Hippolytus—do you know him?   400
By what vain hope do you think he would pity me,
respect in me alone a sex he disdains?
You see how long he has avoided our path,
looking for all the places where we are not.

Ismene

I know what the legend is about his coldness;   405
but I have seen that proud Hippolytus near you,
and when I saw him, the very fame of his pride
doubled my curiosity. His appearance
seemed not at all in keeping with that fame.
I saw him grow confused at your first glance.
His eyes, uselessly trying to avoid you,   410
already full of languor, could not quit you.
The name of lover may offend his bravery,
but he has the eyes of one, if not the speech.

Aricia

How eagerly I listen, dear Ismene,   415
to words perhaps of little substance. You
who know me, should you have thought it credible
that the sad toy of a remorseless fate,
a heart long nourished on tears and bitterness,
could know love, its absurd pain? I alone,   420
last remnant of a king, the noble son
of the earth Goddess, have escaped war's fury.
I lost six brothers in the flower of youth—

what hope of a great lineage! The sword
reaped all that harvest: the moist earth received   425
unwillingly the blood of Erechtheus' heirs.
You know how, since that time, a severe law
forbids all men of Greece to hope for me.
It is feared the reckless ardor of the sister
may call to life, one day, her brothers' ashes.   430
But you know, too, with what scorn I regarded
that watchfulness of a suspicious conqueror.
You know how, steadfastly opposed to love,
I have often given thanks to the harsh Theseus,
whose welcome rigor seconded my pride.   435
But then my eyes, my eyes had not seen his son.
Not that with eyes alone, basely enchanted,
I admire his beauty, his much noted grace,
those gifts conferred by nature to honor him,
which he himself scorns and seems ignorant of.   440
I love, I prize in him less common riches:
his father's virtues, without his weaknesses.
I love, I do confess, that noble pride
which never has endured the yoke of love.
Phaedra had small renown in Theseus' longing.   445
I would have more: I shun the easy triumph
to win a homage that has fallen to thousands,
to invade a heart that's open on all sides.
But to subdue a stubborn will, to strike
pain into an unfeeling soul, to chain   450
a prisoner astonished by his chains,
in futile strife against a pleasing bondage—
that is what I wish, what excites me. Hercules
was easier to disarm than Hippolytus;
vanquished more often, sooner overcome,   455
he brought less glory to the eyes that tamed him.
But, dear Ismene, what recklessness! I shall find
only too much resistance to my will.
Perhaps you will hear me, humble in my misery,
weeping for that same pride I admire today.   460
Hippolytus in love? By what strange good fortune
could I have moved—

Ismene

You will hear him, himself.
He has come to find you.

(Hippolytus enters.)

Hippolytus

Madam, before I leave,
I thought I must advise you of your future.
My father lives no more. My accurate fears   465
foretold the reason of his too long absence.
Death alone, cutting off his brilliant labors,
could hide him from the world so long. The Gods
at last give over to the murdering Fate
Alcides' friend, companion, and successor.   470
I trust your hatred, sparing his true worth,
hears willingly these names which are his due.
My grief is lightened by one hope: I can
release you from an austere guardianship.
I do revoke some strict laws I deplored.   475
You may command yourself—your life, your heart,
and in this Troezen, now my share and once
the heritage of my forefather Pittheus,
which without temporizing has named me king,
I leave you free, and freer than myself.   480

Aricia

Measure the goodness that too much constrains me.
So generously to honor my misfortune,
this is to place me, sir, more than you think,
under those hard laws you suspend for me.

Hippolytus

Athens, debating the succession, speaks   485
of you and of myself, and the Queen's son.

Aricia

Of me, my lord?

Hippolytus

To put aside self-flattery,
I know an insolent law seems to reject me.
I am reproached, by Greece, with a foreign mother.
But if my brother were my only rival,   490

madam, I have some honest rights above him
which I could save from the caprice of laws.
Something more just restrains me: I yield to you—
rather, return to you, a place, a scepter
held by your ancestors in pristine days   495
from that illustrious mortal whom Earth conceived.
By adoption it was placed in Aegeus' hands.
Athens, preserved and strengthened by my father,
acclaimed with joy so honorable a king
and put your unhappy brothers out of mind.   500
Now Athens calls you back within its walls.
Too long it has groaned with quarreling; too long
wasted upon its fields, your family's blood
has nourished the same ground from which it sprang.
Troezen obeys me. The ploughed soil of Crete   505
offers the son of Phaedra a rich home.
Athens is yours. I go to reunite,
for you, the pledges in dispute between us.

Aricia

Surprised and overwhelmed by all I hear,
I am afraid, almost, a dream beguiles me.   510
Am I awake? Can I believe such purpose?
What God, my lord, has placed it in your heart?
How justly is your fame told everywhere,
and how the truth surpasses the renown,
that you, to my advantage, would betray   515
your interest. Was it not enough to refrain
from hating me, to defend your soul so long
against that enmity—

Hippolytus

                        I, hate you, madam?
However cold and proud I have been painted,
is it the legend that a monster bore me?   520
What savage ways, what obdurate ill will
could, seeing you, not become less unkind?
How could I have resisted the baffling charm—

Aricia

What have you said, my lord?

Hippolytus

I have gone too far.
Reason, I see, gives way to urgent feeling.   525
But since I have begun to break the silence,
madam, I must continue. I must share
a secret I can keep at heart no longer.
You see before you a most wretched prince,
a memorable instance of rash pride.   530
I who so long, in arrogant revolt
from love, mocked at its prisoners' iron chains,
who, pitying the shipwreck of weak mortals,
meant always to observe the storms from shore—
now in subjection to that common law,   535
with what surprise I am swept beyond myself!
One moment served to tame my insolence:
this scornful spirit is at last dependent.
For nearly six months hopeless, full of shame,
carrying everywhere the barb that hurts me,   540
with you, and with myself, vainly I strive.
If present, I avoid you; absent, I find you.
Your image moves with me in the deep forest.
The light of day, the shadows of the night,
all summon to my eyes what I avoid,   545
all rival to bring back to you the defiant
Hippolytus; and now, for all my striving,
I seek myself and find myself no more.
All wearies me—my bow, my javelins,
my chariot. I have forsaken Neptune's teaching.   550
Only my deep sighs echo in the wood;
my idle coursers have forgotten my voice.
Perhaps the avowal of so rude a love
makes you ashamed, to be the cause of it.
What poor, rough words to offer you a heart!   555
What a strange captive for so fair a bond!
But the offering should be better prized for this.
Remember, I speak to you in a strange language.
Do not reject the crudely spoken vows
which, but for you, would never have been formed.   560

(Enter Theramenes.)

Theramenes

My lord, the Queen. I have preceded her.
She comes to you.

Hippolytus

　　　　To me?

Theramenes

　　　　　　　I do not know
her purpose, but she has sent to ask for you.
Phaedra would speak with you before you leave.

Hippolytus

Phaedra? What shall I say? What can she hope—　　　565

Aricia

My lord, you cannot well refuse to hear her.
Although too certain of her enmity,
you owe some shadow of pity to her grief.

Hippolytus

Meanwhile you go away. And I must leave,
not knowing if I offend what I most love,　　　570
or if this heart I give in trust to you—

Aricia

Go, Prince. Be constant in your generous plan.
Bring Athens under tribute to my power.
All you have wished to give me I accept.
But that empire—indeed so great, so glorious—　　　575
is not, to me, the dearest of your gifts.

　　　　　　　　(Exeunt Aricia and Ismene.)

Hippolytus

Friend, is all ready? But the Queen comes now.
Let each man be prepared to leave. Go quickly,
order it, give the signal, and return
to save me from a troubling interview.　　　580

　　*(Exit Theramenes. Enter Phaedra and Oenone. During the
　　　　following scene Oenone remains in the background.)*

Phaedra (to Oenone)

He is here. All my blood goes to my heart.
I forget, seeing him, what I came to say.

Oenone

Recall a son whose only hope is in you.

Phaedra

    I am informed you soon take leave of us,
    my lord. To your grief I come to join my tears,   585
    and tell you my anxiety for a son.
    My son has lost a father, and not far
    is the day when he must witness my death, too.
    Even now a thousand foes attack his childhood.
    You, only you, can take his part against them.   590
    But I am deeply troubled by remorse
    unspoken. I fear I have closed your ears to his cries.
    I tremble to reflect that your just anger
    against a hated mother, may fall on him.

Hippolytus

    Madam, my sentiments are not so base.   595

Phaedra

    I should not complain, sir, if you hated me.
    You have seen me diligent to do you mischief.
    My heart you could not deeply read. I have
    deliberately exposed myself to your anger.
    I could not tolerate you on the same shores.   600
    Rejecting you in public and in private,
    I have wished to put the breadth of seas between us.
    I have even forbidden, by a special law,
    that your name be spoken in my hearing. Yet,
    if punishment be measured to the crime,   605
    if only hatred can attract your hatred,
    never was woman, sir, more to be pitied,
    or less deserving of your enmity.

Hippolytus

    Jealous of her own children's due, a mother
    rarely forgives the son of another wife: 610
    I know it, madam. Continual suspicion
    is the most common fruit of second marriage.
    Another would have shown the same mistrust,
    and I, perhaps, should have had more to bear.

Phaedra

    Sir, heaven has wished, I dare attest it here,   615
    to except me from that common law. The care
    that troubles, that consumes me, is most different.

Hippolytus

Madam, it is still early to be troubled.
Your husband may survive all dangers. Heaven,
acceding to our tears, may grant his return.   620
Neptune protects him, and that patron God
will never hear my father's prayer unmoved.

Phaedra

No one sees twice the landing-place of the dead.
Since Theseus has beheld the somber shore,
you hope in vain, sir, for a God to return him;   625
nor does the greedy Acheron loose its prey.
Yet he is not dead, for he breathes in you.
I think I see my husband still. I see him,
I speak to him. My heart. . . . I wander, sir.   630
My insane wish speaks out against my will.

Hippolytus

I see the wonderful effect of your love.
Theseus, though dead, is present to your eyes;
still with his love your soul is warmed and quickened.

Phaedra

Yes, Prince, I am burning, languishing for Theseus.
I love him, not as hell has seen him, the faithless   635
idolator of a sundry thousand, who goes
to desecrate the couch of the God of death—
but chaste, but proud, and even a little stern,
young, charming, in command of every heart,
as our Gods are described, or as I see you.   640
He had your bearing, he had your eyes, your speech:
that noble modesty colored his face,
when he crossed over the waters of our Crete,
fit subject of the prayers of Minos' daughters.
Where were you? Why, without Hippolytus,   645
did he assemble the flower of the Greek heroes?
Why could you not, though but a stripling then,
have stolen into the ship that brought him there?
By you the Cretan monster would have perished,
for all the windings of his vast retreat.   650
To guide you in that devious path my sister
would have forearmed you with the fatal thread.

But no, I should have had the thought before her;
love, first, would have inspired me with the plan.
It is I, Prince, it is I whose precious aid   655
would have made clear to you the turning scheme.
What thought, what care that dear life would have cost me!
A thread would not suffice the one who loves you:
companion of the peril you must seek,
I myself should have gone before you. Phaedra,   660
into the Labyrinth with you descending,
with you would have been rediscovered, or lost.

Hippolytus

What am I hearing? Madam, do you forget
that Theseus is my father and your husband?

Phaedra

Why, Prince, do you suppose I have forgotten?   665
Would I have lost all care for my renown?

Hippolytus

Madam, forgive. I own—I am much distressed—
I have accused in error a blameless word.
My shame can bear your sight no longer. I go—

Phaedra

Ah, cruel, you have understood me too well.   670
I have told enough to leave no risk of error.
Well, then, know Phaedra: all her rage and madness.
I love. Do not believe that while I love you,
guiltless in my own eyes, I approve myself,
or that my weak compliance has fed the poison   675
of the demented love that blurs my reason.
Unlucky object of celestial vengeance,
I loathe myself even more than you detest me.
The Gods know it, those Gods who in my breast
lighted the fire fatal to all my race,   680
those Gods who have made themselves a cruel glory
leading astray the heart of a weak mortal.
Recall to mind the past. It was not enough,
cruel, to fly from you. I hounded you.
I wished you to think me odious, inhuman.   685
More surely to resist you, I sought your hate.
What have my useless efforts profited?

You hated more, I did not love you less.
All your misfortunes lent you a new charm.
I pined, I was consumed, in flames, in tears.   690
Only your eyes were needed to know this,
if once, if for a moment, your eyes could see me.
What do I say? Even this confession, this shameful
confession, do you believe it voluntary?
Uneasy for a son whom I must not fail,   695
I came to entreat your kindness. Weak resolve
of a heart too full of what it loves! Alas,
I could speak to you only of yourself.
Take your revenge. Punish a hateful love.
You, worthy son of the hero who gave you life,   700
deliver the world from a monster that annoys you.
The widow of Theseus dares to love his son!
Believe, this frightful monster must not escape you.
Here is my heart. It is here your hand must strike.
Already impatient to expiate its offense,   705
I feel it straining forward to meet your hand.
Strike. If you think it unworthy of your thrust,
if your hate grudges me so kind a torture,
if your hand would be drenched with blood too vile
and will not serve me, lend me your sword now.   710
Let it be done.
(*She snatches Hippolytus' sword and is about to stab herself
        when Oenone runs forward and struggles with her.*)
Oenone
                What now, my lady? Just Gods!
Someone is coming. Avoid hateful eyes;
return with me. Come, fly from certain shame.
                (*Exeunt Phaedra and Oenone. Enter Theramenes.*)
Theramenes
Is it Phaedra hastening, or hastened, away?
But why, my lord, this stricken look? I see you   715
without your sword—stunned, pale.
Hippolytus
                                Theramenes,
let us go quickly. I am badly shaken.
I cannot even regard myself without fear.

149

Phaedra . . . No, by the Gods! May all that horror
be buried deeply in forgetfulness.   720

Theramenes

The fleet is standing by, if you wish to sail.
But Athens, sir, already has declared.
Its leaders have conferred with all the tribes:
your brother wins. Phaedra is in control.

Hippolytus

Phaedra?

Theramenes

        A herald charged with Athens' will   725
has come to put the State's power in her hands.
Her son is king, my lord.

Hippolytus

               Gods, you who know her,
is it her virtue, then, you recompense?

Theramenes

Meanwhile a rumor has it that the King lives:
they tell of seeing Theseus in Epirus.   730
But I who searched for him, I know too well—

Hippolytus

No matter; we will hear everything, slight nothing.
Let us examine that rumor, go to its source.
If it does not warrant interrupting my journey,
we sail: our purpose, at whatever cost,   735
to put the scepter in hands fit to hold it.

ACT THREE

(*Enter Phaedra and Oenone.*)

Phaedra

Let them go elsewhere with the honors they bring.
Importunate woman, would you have me seen?
What flattery do you bring my wretched spirit?
Hide me, rather: I have but too much spoken.   740
My crazed passions have dared to run at large.
I have said what no one should have heard. Ah, heaven,
how he listened to me! How long, by what twists and turns,
the stony-hearted creature eluded my words!
How he was panting to be gone, and how   745
the red flush of his cheek doubled my shame!
Why did you turn me from my deadly wish?
Alas! When his sword was groping for my heart,
did he turn pale for me? Did he wrest it from me?
Enough that I had touched it once: I had made   750
it horrible in his inhuman eyes,
and that unlucky blade would defile his hand.

Oenone

So, in misfortune pitying yourself,
you tend and feed a fire that should be quenched.
Would it not be better, child of the proud blood   755
of Minos, to seek your rest in nobler cares,
to fly from an ingrate who attracts you—to reign,
and give yourself to conduct of the State?

Phaedra

I, reign? I, range a state under my law,
when my poor mind no longer reigns in me,   760
when I have lost the empire of my senses
and scarcely breathe under a shameful yoke!
When I am dying!

Oenone

                    Fly.

Phaedra

                I cannot leave him.

Oenone

You dared to banish, you dare not avoid him?

Phaedra

It is too late. He knows my insane longing.   765
The bounds of rigid decency are passed.
I have bared my shame to my subjugator, and hope,
against my will, has stolen into my heart.
You yourself, when you rallied my failing strength,
my soul already wandering on my lips,   770
were able to revive me with flattering words.
You let me imagine, then, that I could love him.

Oenone

Alas, guilty or innocent of your sorrows,
what was I not prepared to do, to save you?
But if ever insolence hurt you to the quick,   775
can you forget the scorn of a haughty man?
With what hard eyes, what wilful unconcern,
he let you all but fling yourself at his feet.
Ah, his grim pride made him odious! Why could not
Phaedra, but for that moment, see with my eyes?   780

Phaedra

Oenone, he may put off that wounding pride.
Reared in the wilderness, he has its rudeness.
Hardened by savage ways, Hippolytus
hears speech of human love for the first time.
It may be his surprise that caused his silence,   785
and we complain, perhaps, too much.

Oenone

                          Remember,
the womb of a barbarian conceived him.

Phaedra

A Scythian and barbarian, yet she loved.

Oenone

He is predestined to hate all the sex.

Phaedra

Then I shall see no rival preferred to me.   790

In short, your counsels are no longer timely.
Serve my madness, Oenone, not my reason.
His heart is inaccessible to love:
Then let us strike where he is sensitive.
The charms of an empire have appeared to touch him.   795
Athens attracted him, he could not hide it;
already he had pointed his vessels there,
and the sails floated on the wind outspread.
Go find on my behalf that ambitious youth,
Oenone. Make the crown glitter in his eyes.   800
Let him wear the sacred diadem; I would have
no honor but to place it on his brow.
Let us yield to him this power I cannot keep.
He will rear my son in the commander's art;
perhaps he will take a father's place for him.   805
I entrust both son and mother to his power.
Try, at last, every means to bend him: your words
will find more credit than mine. Urge, weep, bewail
Phaedra about to die, nor blush to take
a suppliant tone. I will consent to all,   810
acknowledge all. My last hope is in you.
Go. I await you, to decide my end.

(Exit Oenone.)

Phaedra (alone)

O you who see to what shame I have come,
implacable Venus, am I enough confounded?
You could no further push your cruelty.   815
Your triumph is perfect; all your shafts go home.
Unmerciful, if you would have new glory,
strike at a more rebellious enemy.
Hippolytus flies from you; braving your anger,
not once has bent his knees before your altars.   820
Your name seems to annoy his haughty ears.
Goddess, avenge yourself: we have one cause.
Cause him to love.

(Enter Oenone.)

　　　　　　But you return so soon,
Oenone? I am detested. He will not hear you.

Oenone

My lady, you must stifle a vain love.   825
Recall your virtue of the past. The King,
who was thought dead, will soon appear to you.
Theseus arrives. He is already near.
The running crowds press round him. As I was going
at your command to find Hippolytus   830
the triumph of a thousand cries went up—

Phaedra

My husband is alive. No more, Oenone.
I have told the unworthy secret of a love
outraging him. He lives: I would hear no more.

Oenone

What?

Phaedra

     I foretold it, but you would not have it.   835
Your tears prevailed over my just repentance.
I lay near death at morning, worthy of grief.
I have followed your advice: I die dishonored.

Oenone

You die?

Phaedra

     Just heaven! What have I done today?
My husband here, with his son! I shall see   840
the cold witness of my adulterous flame
observing with what face I greet his father—
heart full of sighs, which he refused to hear,
eyes wet with tears, by the ingrate despised.
Do you suppose, mindful of Theseus' honor,   845
he will conceal from him my burning love?
Will he see his father and his king betrayed?
Can he contain his horror? But he would be
silent in vain. I know my perfidies,
Oenone. I am not of those bold women   850
who can live tranquilly in crime, who learn
to fashion for themselves an unblushing face.
I know my madnesses, I remember all.
Even now it seems to me these walls, these arches
are about to speak, are ready to accuse me,   855

154

are waiting for my husband, to undeceive him.
Let us die. From so much horror may death release me.
Is it such great misfortune to live no more?
For the unhappy, dying holds no fear.
I have one fear: the name I leave behind me. 860
For my sad children, what a heritage!
The blood of Jupiter should give them courage,
but for all the pride such handsome blood inspires,
a mother's infamy is a grave burden.
I fear some story—alas, too true—one day 865
will taunt them with a mother's guilt. I fear
neither the one nor the other, overborne
by that odious weight, will dare lift up his eyes.

Oenone

In truth I pity them, the one and the other;
never was fear more reasonable than yours. 870
But why expose them to such insolence? Why
bear witness against yourself? The end is certain:
it will be said that Phaedra, all too guilty,
flies from the fearful look of her wronged husband.
Hippolytus will rejoice that you yourself, 875
dying, confirm his story at cost of life.
What can I say to answer your accuser?
Before him, I shall be easy to confound.
I shall see him taste his horrible triumph, tell
your shame to any that will listen. Ah, 880
rather the flaming wrath of heaven devoured me!
But do not mock me: Is he still dear to you?
In what light do you see that audacious prince?

Phaedra

I see a monster, revolting to my eyes.

Oenone

Then why concede him a perfect victory? 885
You fear him. Dare to charge him first with the crime
for which he can denounce you at this moment.
Who will give you the lie? All speaks against him:
his sword left fortunately in your hands,
your present agitation, your past suffering, 890

155

his father warned by your complaints so long,
his former exile by yourself obtained.
Phaedra

I, dare to oppress and blacken innocence?
Oenone

My zealous will needs but your silence. Like you,
I tremble, I have some remorse. You would find me   895
more willing to confront a thousand deaths.
But since I lose you without this sad relief,
your life, for me, is precious above all.
I will speak. Theseus, though my words provoke him,
will limit his revenge to his son's exile.   900
A father, punishing, is still a father:
a light affliction satisfies his anger.
Yet should the blood of innocence be spilled,
what does your threatened honor not demand?
It is too dear a treasure to compromise.   905
Whatever it imposes must be borne:
All, madam, all, to save your hard-pressed honor,
be sacrificed, even virtue.—They are coming.
I can see Theseus.
Phaedra

              I see Hippolytus,   910
my downfall written in his insolent eyes.
Do as you will, I am in your hands. In this
dismay I can do nothing for myself.

          (*Enter Theseus, with Hippolytus and Theramenes.*)
Theseus

Fortune opposes my desire no longer,
madam, and to your arms has brought—   915
Phaedra

                     No, Theseus,
do not profane this charming exaltation.
I am no longer worth these fond regards.
You are offended. In your absence, fortune,
a jealous fortune, has not spared your wife.   920
Unfit to please, to approach you, I must have
no thought hereafter but to hide myself.

              (*Exeunt Phaedra and Oenone.*)

Theseus
　What is this strange reception for your father,
　my son?
Hippolytus
　　　　　Phaedra alone can solve that mystery.　925
　But if my earnest wish has power to move you,
　be pleased, sir, that I do not see her again.
　Grant that Hippolytus may, in dread, be gone
　forever from the place your wife inhabits.
Theseus
　You, my son, leave me?　930
Hippolytus
　　　　　　I did not seek her out:
　it was you that led her to this coast. In leaving,
　it was your final pleasure to entrust
　to the shores of Troezen, Aricia and the Queen.
　I was even given the care of guarding them.　935
　But now, sir, what can hold me? Long enough,
　wandering in the forests, my idle youth
　has shown its skill against indifferent foes.
　Shall I not fly from an unworthy rest
　and stain my javelins with more glorious blood?
　When you were younger than I am today,
　more than one tyrant, more than one fierce monster
　had known the full weight of your arm; even then,
　fortunate persecutor of insolence,　940
　you had made safe the shores of the two seas.
　The traveler freely ranged, and feared no more.
　Hercules, on the strength of your renown,
　took respite from his labors, trusting in you.
　And I, unknown son of so great a father,　945
　have yet to rival even my mother's daring.
　Grant that my courage may at last be used.
　Grant that, if any monster has escaped you,
　I bring its honorable hide to your feet—
　or that the lasting fame of a good death,　950
　recalling endlessly a life well ended,
　may prove me, to the universe, your son.

157

Theseus

What do I see? What spreading horror here
makes my distracted family fly from me?
If I return so feared, so little welcome,   955
why, heaven, did you release me from my prison?
I had but one friend. It was his mad wish
to abduct the Epirotic tyrant's wife.
I served against my will his lusty plan,
but fate, in anger, blinded us. The tyrant   960
caught me without defense, unarmed. I saw
Pirithous, helpless object of my tears,
thrown by that barbarous king to cruel monsters
whose strength he nourished on the blood of men.
Myself he imprisoned in unlighted caverns,   965
deep places near the kingdom of the dead.
After six months the Gods at last were mindful:
I managed to deceive the eyes that watched.
I purged creation of a treacherous foe;
he was himself a pasture to his beasts.   970
And now when joyfully I think to clasp
all that is dearest of what the Gods have left,
now when my soul, which claims itself once more,
has come to feast upon that cherished sight,
I find no welcome but strange fearful looks: 975
all fly from me, all shrink from my embraces.
And I myself, feeling the dread I inspire,
would be again in the prisons of Epirus.
Speak. Phaedra complains that I am wronged.
Who wronged me? Why am I not avenged? Has Greece,   980
to whom my arm so many times was useful,
given some refuge to the criminal?
You do not say. Does my son, my own son,
treat with my enemies? Let us go in.
This doubt too much afflicts me. Let us know   985
at once the guilty deed and the guilty man.
Let Phaedra show the cause of her troubled state.

(*Exit Theseus.*)

Hippolytus (*to Theramenes*)

What was behind those words that chilled me with fear?

158

Does Phaedra, still the prey of her strange madness,
wish to accuse and damn herself? By the Gods,   990
what will the King say? What a fatal poison
the power of love has spread through all his house!
I, too, full of a longing he reproves—
think what I used to be, and how he finds me.
Some dark presentiments come to dismay me.   995
But innocence, all said, has nothing to fear.
Let's go apart and find some happy skill
to enlist my father's sympathy and tell him
of a love which, though he wish to trouble it,
not all his power could even slightly shake.   1000

ACT FOUR

(*Enter Theseus and Oenone.*)

Theseus

What do I hear? A traitor, a rash brute,
conceived this outrage to his father's honor?
How sternly, fate, you press me! I do not know
where I am going, I do not know where I am.
O tender care! O kindness ill rewarded!   1005
Audacious plan! Abominable thought!
To attain the object of his shameful love
he did not scruple to use force. I know
the blade, the instrument of his lust, that blade
with which I armed him for a nobler use.   1010
Not all the ties of blood could give him pause?
And Phaedra delayed still to have him punished?
Phaedra, in silence, spared the criminal?

Oenone

Phaedra spared rather a most injured father.
In shame to have caused his brutal, crazed desire,   1015
the wild flame of his look, she was resolved
to die, my lord. Phaedra's destroying hand
would have put out the clear light of her eyes.
I saw her arm uplifted. I ran to save her.
Thus only was she saved to you; and in pity   1020
for her distress and yours, I dared to speak,
against my will, interpreting her tears.

Theseus

False heart! I do not wonder he turned pale.
I saw his look of terror when we met.
I was astonished by his lack of joy;   1025
his cold embraces put my fondness off.
But had that guilty love which preys on him
even before, in Athens, declared itself?

160

Oenone
> My lord, remember the complaints of the Queen.
> A criminal desire caused all her hate.   1030

Theseus
> And here in Troezen it flared up anew?

Oenone
> My lord, I have told you all that happened. The Queen
> remains too much alone with her mortal grief.
> Now suffer me to leave you and go to her.
>
> > (*Exit Oenone. Enter Hippolytus.*)

Theseus
> Ah, here he is! Great Gods, by that noble bearing,   1035
> what eye would not, like mine, have been deceived?
> Why, then, must a profane adulterer's face
> shine with the sacred character of virtue?
> Should we not recognize by certain signs
> the hearts of treacherous men?

Hippolytus
> > May I inquire   1040
> what fateful cloud, my lord, has overcast
> the brow of majesty? Will you not dare
> confide that secret to my loyalty?

Theseus
> Traitor! You dare to show yourself before me?
> Ill creature, whom the lightning spares too long,   1045
> foul remnant of the thieves I have scoured from earth!
> After the transport of a horrible love
> has pushed its madness even to your father's bed,
> you dare to rear before me a hostile face,
> you stand in the very haunts of your infamy   1050
> and do not go to seek, under some far sky,
> unheard-of lands my name may not have reached.
> Go, traitor. Do not come to brave my hate
> and tempt an anger I control with pain.
> I am enough, and for all time, dishonored,   1055
> to have put on earth so criminal a son,
> without your death to heap new shame upon me
> and soil the glory of my noble works.
> Go: if you would not instantly be numbered

with the great scoundrels I have punished, take care 1060
that you are never seen by the sun that lights us
to set a bold and lawless foot in this place.
Go, I say: speeding your steps without return,
purge all my states of your abhorrent sight.
And you, Neptune, and you, if once my courage 1065
swept clean your coast of infamous assassins,
remember, as the prize of my success,
you promised to accord me my first wish.
Through the long rigors of a cruel prison,
not once have I implored your deathless power. 1070
Miserly of the help I await from you,
my prayers reserved you for more serious needs.
I implore you now. Revenge a suffering father.
I yield this traitor to your total wrath.
Drown in his blood his insolent desires: 1075
let Theseus, by your fury, know your kindness.
Hippolytus
Phaedra accuses me of a criminal love!
Horror in such profusion stuns my soul;
so many blows, so unforeseen, come down,
I am bereft of speech, my voice is stifled. 1080
Theseus
False-hearted one, you imagined she would bury
your brutal insult in a cowardly silence.
You should not have abandoned, as you fled,
the sword which in her hand serves to condemn you;
or, making whole your treachery with one thrust, 1085
you should have ravished from her both speech and life.
Hippolytus
In righteous anger at so black a lie,
I should let truth be spoken here, my lord,
but I suppress what deeply touches you.
Think well of the respect that keeps me silent; 1090
rather than wishing to increase your pain,
look at my life, consider what I am.
Some crimes always precede the major crimes.
Whoever dares beyond the lawful bounds

may at last violate the holiest rights;   1095
even as virtue, crime has its degrees;
and never has shy innocence been seen
to pass abruptly to the extreme of license.
Not in a day are virtuous men made prone
to sly and faithless murder, to cowardly incest. 1100
I, reared and taught by a chaste heroine,
have not betrayed her divine blood. From her,
Pittheus, known as wisest among men,
deigned to receive me, for my further teaching.
I would not show myself too favorably,   1105
but if any strength has fallen to my lot,
I think, sir, I have proved above all else
my hatred of these crimes now laid to me.
For this Hippolytus is known in Greece.
I have carried virtue to the point of harshness. 1110
All have observed my stubborn will; in this
my heart is candid as the light of day.
And it is said that I, in profane lust—
Theseus
Yes, it is this same pride, coward, condemns you.
I see the ugly principle of your coldness: 1115
Phaedra alone charmed your licentious eyes;
indifferent to all others, you disdained
to feel an innocent desire.
Hippolytus
       No, Father,
my heart—it is too much to hide from you—
has not disdained to feel a virtuous love.   1120
I acknowledge at your feet my true offense:
I love. I love, indeed, against your law.
Aricia has my promise, my obedience;
your son is conquered by the child of Pallas.
I worship her, and my rebellious soul   1125
can have no thought, no longing, but for her.
Theseus
Do you, by heaven? But no: the device is crude.
You assume a villainy to clear yourself.

Hippolytus

    For six months I have fled from her and loved her.
    I came, quite anxiously, to tell you this.   1130
    What, then? Will nothing move you from your error?
    By what tremendous oath can I assure you?
    Let earth and heaven be witness, let all nature—

Theseus

    The scoundrels always have recourse to perjury.
    Enough, enough: spare me a long harangue,   1135
    if your false virtue has no other prop.

Hippolytus

    It appears false to you and full of guile.
    In her heart, Phaedra does me greater justice.

Theseus

    Ah, how your impudence stirs up my wrath!

Hippolytus

    How long shall I be exiled? In what place?   1140

Theseus

    Were you beyond the pillars of Hercules,
    I should still think myself too near a traitor.

Hippolytus

    Charged with the fearful crime you impute to me,
    what friends will pity me when you reject me?

Theseus

    Go look for friends whose ruinous esteem   1145
    bows to adultery and applauds incest,
    false, thankless creatures without honor or law,
    fit to protect a miscreant such as you.

Hippolytus

    You speak still of adultery and incest?
    I will not reply. Yet as her mother's child   1150
    Phaedra is of a blood, you know too well,
    more plentiful in all those horrors than mine.

Theseus

    What? You abandon all restraint before me?
    Now for the last time, rid me of your sight.
    Go, traitor. Do not force an incensed father
    to have you miserably dragged from here.   1155

                          (*Exit Hippolytus.*)

Theseus (alone)
Unhappy wretch, you go to your certain doom.
By that river terrible even to the Gods,
Neptune gave me his word, and will perform it.
An avenging God pursues. You cannot escape.   1160
I loved you; and, in spite of your offense,
I feel my vitals wrung in that foreknowledge.
But you have too much forced me to condemn you.
In truth, was any father more deeply wronged?
Just Gods, who see the grief that overcomes me,   1165
can I have put on earth so guilty a child?
                              (*Enter Phaedra.*)
Phaedra
My lord, I have come to you in just alarm.
Your terrifying voice has reached me. I fear
a hasty action may have followed the threat.
If there is time still, spare your lineage.   1170
Respect your blood, I dare implore you; save me
from hearing it cry out, from the horrible noise
of its crying. Spare me the eternal pain
of causing it to flow by a father's hand.
Theseus
No, madam, my hand is free of my own blood.   1175
Yet the ungrateful life has not escaped me.
An immortal hand is charged with his ruin: Neptune
owes it to me, and you shall be avenged.
Phaedra
Neptune owes it to you! Your excited prayers—
Theseus
What? Do you fear, so soon, they will be heard?   1180
Join, rather, in my lawful prayers; retrace
his crimes to me in all their sordidness;
rechafe my too slow, too much bridled anger.
Not all his crimes are known to you as yet:
his rage pours out in calumnies against you.   1185
He says your mouth is full of sly deceits,
declares Aricia has his heart, his promise,
that he loves her.

Phaedra
>   What, sir?
Theseus
>   He told me so.
> But that's a trifling artifice: I reject it.
> Let us hope now for justice from the God.   1190
> I go myself to kneel before his altars
> and urge him to fulfil his deathless vow.

>   (*Exit Theseus.*)
Phaedra (*alone*)
> He has gone away. What news has struck my ear?
> What flame, only half stifled, wakes in my heart?
> What lightning bolt, O heaven! What deadly knowledge!   1195
> I ran wholeheartedly to his son's aid;
> freeing myself from terrified Oenone,
> I had given way to the remorse that wrung me.
> Who knows where that repentance would have led?
> I might have been prepared to accuse myself;   1200
> before my voice was stopped, I might have blurted
> the execrable truth. Hippolytus
> has power to feel, and feels nothing for me!
> Aricia has his heart, his pledge! Ah, Gods,
> when the unbudging creature against my prayers   1205
> put on so proud an eye, so stern a front,
> I thought his heart still shut away from love,
> equally shielded against all my sex.
> And yet another has tamed his arrogance;
> in his cruel eyes another has found grace.   1210
> Perhaps his heart is easily made tender:
> I am the single object he cannot bear;
> and I would charge myself with defending him?

>   (*Enter Oenone.*)
> Do you know, my dear Oenone, what I have learned?
Oenone
> No, but in truth I shudder. I went pale   1215
> to think what you intended when you left me:
> I feared a rashness fatal to yourself.

166

Phaedra
  Oenone, who would have imagined it?
  I had a rival.
Oenone
             What?
Phaedra
             Hippolytus loves.
  I cannot doubt it. That tameless enemy   1220
  whom respect offended, human suffering bored,
  that tiger I could not approach without fear—
  submissive, fawning, recognizes a conqueror:
  Aricia has spied out the way to his heart.
Oenone
  Aricia?
Phaedra
             Ah, agony still unexperienced!   1225
  And it was for this torment I saved myself!
  All I have suffered, my fears, my ecstasies,
  frenzy of longing, horror of remorse,
  intolerable insult of rejection,
  were but a weak foreshadowing of this torment.   1230
  They love! By what charm have they tricked my eyes?
  How have they seen each other? Where? Since when?
  You knew. Why did you let me be deceived?
  Could you not tell me of their furtive love?
  Have they been often seen to meet, to speak?   1235
  Where did they hide? In the deep woods? Alas,
  they saw each other with impunity.
  Heaven blessed their innocent desire; they followed
  the leaning of their hearts without remorse;
  day after day rose calm and clear for them.   1240
  And I, sorrowful outcast from all nature,
  hid myself from the morning, fled the light.
  Death was the only God I dared to implore.
  Living but for the moment of my last breath,
  nourished with gall, slaked upon tears, and still   1245
  too closely watched in my unhappiness,
  I dared not drown in weeping as I would;

167

I tasted tremblingly that mournful pleasure—
under a calm face hiding my distress,
often, indeed, deprived myself of tears.   1250
Oenone
What profit will they have of their vain love?
They will not meet again.
Phaedra
                              They will love forever.
This moment, as I speak—ah, mortal thought—
they brave the fury of a love-maddened woman.
Despite that exile which must separate them,   1255
they make a thousand promises. No, no,
I cannot bear a happiness that insults me,
Oenone. Have pity on my jealous rage.
Aricia must be lost. My husband's anger
must be revived against an odious blood.   1260
Let him not rest at a light punishment:
the sister's crime is greater than the brothers'.
In my jealous passion I would urge, implore him.
What am I saying? Where will my reason wander?
I, jealous! And it is Theseus I implore!   1265
My husband lives, and I am burning still—
for whom? To whom do I aspire? Each word
I speak makes my hair rise. Now and henceforth
my crimes have reached to the full brimming measure.
I breathe, at the same moment, guile and incest.   1270
My life-destroying hands, quick for revenge,
are burning to be plunged in innocent blood.
Miserable! And I live, and can bear the eye
of that holy Sun from whom I am descended?
My grandfather is master of the Gods;   1275
my ancestors crowd heaven, the universe.
Where hide? Let's fly into the night of hell.
But no. There my father holds the fatal urn
in his strict hands: they say it is his lot.
There Minos judges each pale human traveler.   1280
Ah, how my shade will tremble when he sees
his daughter led before his eyes, constrained
to avow such grave and various trespasses,

and crimes perhaps unknown in hell. My father,
what will you say to that hair-raising show?   1285
I see the terrible urn fall from your hand;
I see you searching for a new punishment,
become the executioner of your blood.
Forgive. A cruel God has undone your race;
see in your daughter's passion a God's vengeance.   1290
Alas, of the dreadful crime whose shame pursues me,
my joyless heart has never plucked the fruit.
To the last sigh attended by misfortune,
I render up in torment a painful life.

Oenone

No, madam, reject a baseless terror: see   1295
in another light your pardonable fault.
You love. No one surmounts his destiny.
By a fatal spell you were led on and on.
Is it a prodigy unknown among us?
Has love yet triumphed over none but you?   1300
Weakness is all too natural to the human.
You are a mortal: accept a mortal's fate.
The burden under which you cry was imposed
long since. The Gods, even, dwellers on Olympus,
who with such fearful noise appall our crimes,   1305
they, too, have sometimes burned with illicit fires.

Phaedra

What now? What counsel does one dare to give me?
So, to the end, you would instil your poison,
unhappy woman? Thus you ruined me.
When I fled the light, it was you that turned me back.   1310
Your pleading made me forget my duty. I shunned
Hippolytus: it was you that made me see him.
What did you undertake? Accusing him,
how dared your impious mouth blacken his life?
He will die, perhaps. The sacrilegious prayer   1315
of a crazed father is perhaps fulfilled.
I do not listen. Go, execrable monster.
Leave me the care of my most grievous fate.
May the just heaven pay you worthily.
And may your punishment forever frighten   1320

all those who, like yourself, with cowardly art
nourish the frailty of unlucky princes,
push them upon the leaning where they incline,
and dare to smooth for them the unlawful road:
detestable flatterers, the most deadly gift   1325
heaven's anger can bestow on kings!

(*Exit.*)

Oenone (*alone*)

                                   Ah, Gods,
to serve her I have done all, forsaken all.
And this is my reward? I have well deserved it.

ACT FIVE

(Enter Hippolytus and Aricia.)

Aricia
What? You are silent in this mortal danger?
You let a father, who loves you, be deceived?   1330
Cruel, if you scorn the power of my tears,
if you are willing not to see me again,
go, and live far away from sad Aricia,
but at least, in going, make certain of your life.
Defend your honor from a base reproach,   1335
and force your father to retract his vow.
For there is time still. Why, by what caprice,
do you leave an open field to your accuser?
Enlighten Theseus.

Hippolytus
                    What have I not told him?
Should I have let the insult to his bed   1340
cry out? Should I have spoken without reserve
and brought the ignoble blush to a father's face?
No one but you has looked into that mystery.
I can entrust it only to you and the Gods.
I could not hide from you—know, then, I love you—   1345
this secret I have wished to hide from myself.
But remember under what seal I have bared it.
Forget, if it may be, I have spoken to you,
and may such pure lips, madam, never repeat
this horrible surprise. Let us be bold   1350
to place our confidence in the Gods' justice:
it is indeed their interest to defend me;
and Phaedra, punished soon or late for her crimes,
cannot escape just infamy. This alone,
this much of deference, I require of you.   1355
In all the rest I give my anger its way.

171

Rise from the servitude in which you are held,
and join my fortunes: dare to come with me
away from this profaned, ill-omened place
where virtue breathes a poisoned air. To hide   1360
your sudden disappearance you may profit
from the confusion my disgrace has caused.
I can provide the certain means of flight.
You have had, till now, no other guards than mine.
Some great defenders will take up our quarrel;   1365
Argos is open-armed, Sparta invites us:
let us commit our just cause to our friends,
or Phaedra, gathering up our lost estates,
will drive us both from the paternal throne
to assure her son the remnants of our power.   1370
The time is favorable: we must embrace it.
Why do you seem to fear? Do you doubt at all?
Only your interest makes me brave to do it.
Why, when my hope takes fire, do you turn to ice?
Are you afraid to share an exile's fate?   1375

Aricia
Such banishment, my lord, would be most welcome.
With what delight, bound to your destiny,
I should live unremembered by all men!
But since we are not so bound, so dearly bound,
can I, in honor, steal away with you?   1380
I know, without offending strictest honor,
I can release myself from your father's hands:
that would not be to leave my home and kinsmen;
flight is permitted when we fly from tyrants.
But you, sir, love me; and to risk my name. . . .   1385

Hippolytus
No, no, I have too much care for your renown.
I come before you with a nobler plan:
fly from your enemies, but follow your husband.
Free in adversity, since heaven ordains it,
our pledges stand upon no human law.   1390
A wedding is not always ringed about
with torches. At the gates of Troezen, among
those old tombs for the princes of my race,

172

a sacred temple stands, dreadful to perjurers. 1395
There mortals dare not take an oath in vain.
There the disloyal man is swiftly punished,
and, fearing certain death upon that ground,
falsehood has no more terrible restraint.
There, if you trust me, we will go to bind 1400
the vow of an enduring love; we will pray
the Deity who is worshiped there to hear us,
that he may serve as father to us both.
I will invoke the highest names of heaven:
the chaste Diana, the imperial Juno, 1405
and indeed all the Gods, as witnesses,
shall know the honor of my sacred vows.

Aricia

The King is coming. Prince, take leave at once.
I stay a moment to conceal my flight.
Go now, and let some faithful guide remain,
who will direct my frightened steps to you. 1410

(*Exit Hippolytus. Ismene appears and goes to Aricia.
Enter Theseus.*)

Theseus

Gods, help my troubled mind. Be it your will
to show the truth I have come here to seek.

Aricia

Look to all, dear Ismene. Prepare to leave.

(*Exit Ismene.*)

Theseus

Your color changes and you look surprised,
madam. What was Hippolytus doing here? 1415

Aricia

My lord, he bade me an eternal farewell.

Theseus

So, then, your eyes have tamed that defiant heart,
and his first love sighs are your happy work.

Aricia

My lord, I cannot well deny the truth:
he has not inherited your unjust hatred; 1420
he has not used me like a criminal.

Theseus

    I see: he swore you an eternal love.
    Do not rely on that inconstant heart;
    he has sworn as much to others.

Aricia

                    He, my lord?

Theseus

    You should have taught him to be less unsteady.   1425
    How could you have abided that horrible sharing?

Aricia

    And how can you abide the horrible tales
    that dare to blacken so excellent a life?
    Do you know his heart so little? Do you judge
    so indifferently of crime and innocence?   1430
    Must hatred overcloud to you alone
    his virtue that is splendid in all eyes?
    Ah, that is to betray him to false tongues!
    Do it no more: repent your murderous wish;
    fear, my lord, fear, that stern impartial heaven   1435
    may be enough unfriendly to accord it.
    Often, in its anger, it receives our victims;
    often its gifts are judgments for our crimes.

Theseus

    No, you try vainly to obscure his deed.
    Love blinds you in his favor. But I have trust   1440
    in sure and irreproachable witnesses:
    I have seen, seen, those unaffected tears.

Aricia

    Beware, my lord. Your overpowering hand
    has rid the world of countless monsters; but all
    are not destroyed: you permit one to live.   1445
    Your son, my lord, forbids me to go on.
    Well-taught in the respect he keeps for you,
    I should too much offend him by saying more.
    I copy his restraint and leave your presence,
    that I may not be forced to break the silence.   1450

                              (Exit Aricia.)

Theseus (alone)

    What is her meaning? What do those words hide,

so many times begun, always cut short?
Would they confuse me with a vain pretense?
Do they conspire to keep me in this torture?
Here, too, in spite of sternest resolution,   1455
what plaintive voice cries here, deep in my heart?
A secret pity grieves me and dismays me.
Oenone must be questioned once again.
Upon the whole crime I would have more light.
Guards, call Oenone. Let her come alone.   1460

(*Enter Panope.*)

Panope
I do not know what the Queen is meditating,
but all's to fear, my lord, from her present wildness.
She has a mortal, desperate look; the white
shadow of death is even now in her face.
Already, driven from her presence in shame,   1465
Oenone has flung herself in the deep sea.
What caused her frenzy is unknown; and now
the waves have snatched her from our sight forever.
Theseus
What do I hear?
Panope
                    Her death has not calmed the Queen:
the trouble seems to grow in her restless soul.   1470
At times, to soothe her still unspoken grief,
she takes her children, bathes them with her tears,
then suddenly, renouncing maternal love,
she pushes them away from her in horror.
She goes at random with uncertain steps;   1475
her staring eyes no longer know us. Three times
she has begun to write and, her mood changing,
three times has torn apart her unfinished letter.
Sir, deign to see her and to comfort her.
Theseus
Oenone dead, and Phaedra wishes to die?   1480
Call back my son. Let him defend himself.
Let him come speak: I am prepared to hear him.
O Neptune, do not hasten your deadly favors;
I would rather be denied forever. Perhaps

I have too much believed false witnesses, 1485
and lifted up too soon my cruel hands.
Ah, what depair would follow what I have asked!
     (*Exit Panope. Enter Theramenes.*)
Is it you, Theramenes? Where is my son?
I have trusted him from the most tender age
to you. But from what source do those tears flow? 1490
What keeps my son?
Theramenes
     O late, superfluous care!
Most idle tenderness! He is no more.
Theseus
Gods!
Theramenes
    I have seen the most gracious of mortals perish;
I think, too, the least guilty.
Theseus
      My son is dead?
Why, then, when I hold out my arms to him, 1495
the impatient Gods have hastened to cut him down?
What ravished him from me? What lightning stroke?
Theramenes
We had scarcely passed beyond the gates of Troezen.
He was in his chariot. His dejected guards
copied his silence, in their places round him. 1500
Pensive, he followed the Mycenaen road,
letting the reins fall idly on his horses.
Those superb steeds, which in the past one saw,
full of such noble fire, obey his voice,
now with their mournful eyes and bowing heads 1505
seemed to conform to his unhappy mind.
An awful cry, starting below the waves,
pierced suddenly at that moment the quiet air,
and from the depths of earth a mighty voice
responded, groaning, to that ominous cry. 1510
Our blood was frozen in our hearts. The manes
of the attentive horses stood erect.
Meanwhile from the flat sea a watery mountain
rose up in boiling wrath: the billow moved

shoreward, broke, vomited before our eyes   1515
amid the rush of foam, a furious monster,
its wide brow menacingly armed with horns,
all of its body clothed in yellow scales:
a bull untamable, a raging dragon,
twisting away behind in tortuous coils.   1520
Its long roars made the very seacoast shake.
Heaven looked with horror on the savage thing,
earth was aggrieved by it, the air infected.
The wave that carried it withdrew in terror.
Everyone ran; forgetting useless courage,   1525
all sought a refuge in the neighboring temple.
Hippolytus alone, fit son of a hero,
reined in his coursers, drew his javelins,
gave charge, and, launching with a steady hand,
opened a broad wound in the monster's side.   1530
In rage and pain the monster bounded, fell
a-roaring at the horses' feet, rolled over
and opened wide to them its inflamed jaws,
which spewed upon them fire and blood and smoke.
Now terror seized them. Now, unhearing, they strove,   1535
insensible to curb and to command.
Their master spent himself in luckless efforts.
Their mouths foamed red upon the bit. Some say
one could even see, in the dread hurly-burly,
a God stabbing with goads their dusty flanks.   1540
Now up and over the rocks their terror urged them.
The axle screamed and broke. The intrepid prince
saw all his splintered chariot fly in pieces.
He himself, trammeled in the reins, went down.
Excuse my grief. For me, until I die,   1545
that cruel image will be a source of tears.
I saw, my lord, I saw your unhappy son
dragged by the beasts his hand had nourished. He tried
to call them back but his voice startled them.
They ran. Soon his whole body was one wound.   1550
The plain resounded with our stricken cries.
At last their headlong rage was spent: they halted
not far from those archaic tombs where sleep

the cold bones of his royal ancestors.
I ran there, sighing, and his guard followed me.   1555
The trace of his proud blood showed us the way:
the rocks were bright with it, the sickening briers
dangled upon their thorns his gory locks.
I reached him, called him; giving me his hand,
he looked from dying eyes, which straightway closed.   1560
He said: "Heaven rends from me an innocent life.
Take thought, when I am dead, for sad Aricia.
Dear friend, if my father, undeceived some day,
pities the hard fate of a son ill used,
tell him, to quiet my blood, my plaintive ghost,   1565
he must treat his captive gently, restore to her. . . ."
With those words the dead hero left in my arms
but a disfigured body, a piteous thing
where the Gods' anger triumphs, which even the eye
of his father would not recognize.   1570

Theseus
                     O my son,
dear hope I have fiercely severed from myself!
Inexorable Gods, who all too well
have served me! To what remorse my life is doomed!

Theramenes
The shy Aricia at that moment appeared.
She came, my lord, escaping from your anger,   1575
to take him for her husband before the Gods.
She approached: she saw the reddened grass, she saw
Hippolytus lying there, ghastly, distorted.
What object for a lover's eyes! At first
she was unwilling to believe her plight,   1580
not recognizing the brave youth she loved,
and, seeing Hippolytus, still asked for him.
But all too sure, at last, her eyes beheld him,
she accused heaven with a sorrowful look,
and cold, moaning, nearly inanimate,   1585
lies in oblivion at her lover's feet.
Ismene is at her side: Ismene, in tears,
calling her back to life, or rather, pain.

And I—have returned, hating the light,
to inform you of the last wish of a hero,   1590
and to discharge, sir, the unhappy task
which his expiring heart reposed in me.
But I see his mortal enemy approach.
                    (*Enter Phaedra, Panope, and guards.*)
Theseus
So, then, you have prevailed. My son is lifeless.
Ah, I have cause to fear. A cruel doubt,   1595
pleading him in my heart, with cause alarms me.
But, madam, he is dead. Accept your victim:
be happy in his ruin, unjust or lawful.
My eyes would still be blindfolded. I do
believe him criminal, since you accuse him.   1600
His death is enough reason for my tears:
I seek no hateful knowledge, for such knowledge
could not restore him to my natural grief,
and would, perhaps, increase my wretchedness.
Let me go far from you and from this shore,   1605
to flee his bloody, mangled image. Confused
and haunted by a mortal recollection,
I would be exiled from the utmost world.
All seems to rise against me, crying injustice.
My very fame augments my punishment: 1610
less known to mortals, I could better hide.
That interest of the Gods which honors me
I hate. I will go weep their murderous favors,
and trouble them with useless prayers no more.
Whatever they might do, their fatal kindness   1615
could not make good what they have stripped from me.
Phaedra
No, Theseus, I must break an unjust silence:
your son must be given back his innocence.
He was by no means guilty.
Theseus
                    Ah, wretched father!
And I condemned him on your serious word.   1620
Hard woman, do you believe yourself excused—

Phaedra

    Moments are precious to me. Listen, Theseus.
    I myself dared to cast upon that chaste,
    respectful son, profane, incestuous eyes.
    Heaven had placed a killing flame in my heart;   1625
    the detestable Oenone did all the rest.
    She feared Hippolytus, who knew my madness,
    would reveal a passion he had seen with horror.
    The false one, profiting by my grave weakness,
    ran to declare him guilty in your eyes.   1630
    She has paid for it, and, flying from my anger,
    sought in the waves a punishment too kind.
    The sword already would have proved my fate,
    but I left virtue pleading under doubt.
    I have wished, exposing my remorse in your sight,   1635
    to sink more slowly to the dead. I have taken,
    I have let run into my burning veins,
    a poison which Medea brought to Athens.
    So soon it reaches to my heart, instils
    into this dying heart a singular cold.   1640
    Now only through a mist I see the sky
    and the husband whom my presence wrongs; and death,
    stealing the brightness from my eyes, gives back
    to the light, which they defiled, its purity.

Panope

    She is gone, sir.

Theseus

             Would the blackness of her deed   1645
    could die from memory and be gone with her!
    Alas, too well enlightened of my error,
    let us go now and with my poor son's blood
    mingle our tears, embracing what remains,
    to expiate the mad curse I abhor.   1650
    Give him the honors he too well deserved;
    and better to appease his troubled spirit,
    untrue as all her scheming family were,
    may she who loved him be a daughter to me.

A RACINE CHRONOLOGY

1639   Jean Racine born on December 21 at La Ferté-Milon, a town northeast of Paris between Château-Thierry and Soissons; he was named for his father, a district attorney, whose family had been ennobled through a purchased commission. At this time, three years after *Le Cid,* Corneille was thirty-three; Pascal, Molière, and La Fontaine were in their teens; and Louis XIV, still the dauphin, was less than two. The ministry of Richelieu was near its end.

1641   Death of Racine's mother, Jeanne Sconin, on January 28.

1643   Death of his father on February 6. Adoption of Racine by his paternal grandmother, Marie des Moulins. In this year Louis XIV, at the age of five, became king under his mother's regency.

1651   Marie des Moulins went to join her daughter Agnès at the abbey of Port-Royal, where Angélique Arnauld, a friend of the family, was abbess. Racine was sent to the Collège de Beauvais.

1655   He left Beauvais and entered the École des Granges at Port-Royal. Although the famous scholars of the abbey were under persecution for their Jansenism and had been ordered to discontinue the instruction of minors, Racine was permitted to remain as a special student.

1658   He left Port-Royal and entered the Collège d'Harcourt, at Paris, for a year of logic.

1659   Living temporarily with a prosperous cousin, Nicolas Vitart, in the Paris house of the latter's employer, a great duke, he enjoyed some of the pleasures of the city and made the acquaintance of writers, including La Fontaine.

1660   He published *La Nymphe de la Seine,* a poem celebrating the king's marriage, and received a gratification of 100 louis.

1661   He went to visit his uncle, the Chanoine Sconin, vicar general at Uzès, in the south near Nîmes, where he was given the hope of obtaining a clerical appointment. He remained for a year, serving his uncle, but the benefice was not forthcoming.

1662   He returned to Paris at the end of this year or early in 1663. Another occasional poem, *La Renommée aux Muses,* won him another gratification and caught the attention of Boileau, with whom (at this time or later: the evidence is conflicting) he began a lifelong friendship. He devoted himself to playwriting.

1663 He submitted one of two early attempts to Molière, who advised him to destroy it but suggested another subject and advanced him the considerable sum of 100 louis (2,400 French pounds).

1664 His first play, La Thébaïde, was given by Molière's company at the Palais-Royal theater in June.

1665 Alexandre le Grand opened in December at the Palais-Royal. It was soon withdrawn and immediately produced at the Bourgogne, the leading theater for tragedy. The result was a breach between Molière and Racine. He was now being severely reproved by his old friends of Port-Royal, who had taught him to read Sophocles but who execrated the theater. Meantime he fell in love with an actress, Marquise (her first name, not a title) du Parc.

1666 Nicole, the Port-Royal moralist, published his Visionnaires, attacking the theater. Racine replied with two harsh letters against Port-Royal, one of which was published.

1667 Royal preview of Andromaque, his first success, at Versailles in November, and a public opening at the Bourgogne.

1668 His comedy Les Plaideurs opened in November. Death of Mademoiselle du Parc, following a miscarriage, on December 13.

1669 Unlucky opening of Britannicus on December 13.

1670 First performance of Bérénice in November. His affair with the great actress, La Champmeslé, began.

1672 Bajazet opened in January.

1673 Mithridate, which was to be Racine's most popular play in his own time, as well as the king's choice, opened in January. He was received as a member of the Académie Française.

1674 Opening of Iphigénie in August. Racine was appointed treasurer for the royal jurisdiction of Moulins.

1677 Phèdre opened in January and eventually succeeded in spite of a plot to ruin it. Racine decided to leave the theater. He became reconciled with Port-Royal and obtained a co-appointment, with Boileau, as historiographer to the king. On June 1 he married a young woman of excellent family, chosen by his own family and religious counselors, Catherine de Romanet. She was twenty-five, Racine thirty-seven.

1678 Birth of Jean-Baptiste, first of his two sons and five daughters. Racine and Boileau accompanied the king in his campaign against Ypres and Ghent.

1683   They accompanied the king in Alsace.

1687   Racine, sending dispatches to Boileau, followed the royal campaign in Luxembourg.

1689   First performance of *Esther* before the king and a selected court audience, at the Saint-Cyr school for girls, in January.

1691   First performance of *Athalie,* under the same circumstances, at Saint-Cyr in January.

1692   Birth of Louis Racine, his seventh and last child, on November 2.

1693   He began writing his history of Port-Royal Abbey.

1694   Publication of the *Cantiques Spirituels.*

1695   Racine faithfully ministered to La Fontaine in his last illness.

1698   He momentarily incurred the king's displeasure with some outspoken remarks on tyranny.

1699   He died on April 21, at the age of fifty-nine, and was buried at his request in the Port-Royal graveyard beside Hamon, the beloved old physician of the abbey. Twelve years later, when Port-Royal was finally destroyed, his remains were transferred to the Paris church, Saint-Étienne-du-Mont, on the Place du Panthéon, where they rest near those of Pascal.

ENGLISH PRONUNCIATION
OF PROPER NAMES[1]

Acheron   ăk′ēr·ŏn
Agamemnon   ăg′a·měm′nŏn
Agrippina   ăg′rĭ·pī′na
Albina   ăl·bī′na
Alcides   ăl·sī′dēz
Andromache   ăn·drŏm′a·kė̇
Antiope   ăn·tī′ȯ·pė̇
Ariadne   ăr·ĭ·ăd′nė̇
Aricia   a·rĭsh′a
Astyanax   ăs·tī′a·năks
Britannicus   brĭ·tăn′ĭ·kŭs
Burrus   bûr′ŭs
Caligula   ka·lĭg′ů·la
Cephissa   sė̇·fĭs′a
Cercyon   sûr′cĭ·ŏn
Cleone   klė̇·ō′nė̇
Cocytus   kȯ·sī′tŭs
Corbulo   kôr′bů·lō
Domitius   dȯ·mĭsh′ŭs
Elis   ē′lĭs
Epirus   ė̇·pī′rŭs
Erechtheus   ė̇·rĕk′thūs
Germanicus   jûr·măn′ĭ·kŭs
Hecuba   hĕk′ů·ba
Hermione   hûr·mī′ȯ·nė̇
Hippolytus   hĭ·pŏl′ĭ·tŭs
Icarus   ĭk′a·rŭs; ī′ka-
Ismene   ĭs·mē′nė̇

Menelaus   měn·ė̇·lā′ŭs
Minos   mī′nŏs
Mycenaean   mī·sė̇·nē′an
Oenone   ė̇·nō′nė̇
Orestes   ȯ·rĕs′tēz
Otho   ō′thō
Panope   păn′ȯ·pė̇
Pasiphaë   pa·sĭf′a·ē
Phaedra   fē′dra
Pirithous   pī·rĭth′ȯ·ŭs
Piso   pī′sō
Pittheus   pĭt′thūs
Polyxena   pō·lўx′ė̇·na
Procrustes   prȯ·krŭs′tēz
Pylades   pĭl′a·dēz
Pyrrhus   pĭr′ŭs
Sciron   sī′rŏn
Scythian   sĭth′ĭ·ăn
Seneca   sĕn′ė̇·ka
Senecio   sė̇·nē′shĭ·ō
Silanus   sī·lā′nŭs
Sinis   sĭn′ĭs
Taenarus   tē′na·rŭs
Theramenes   thė̇·răm′ė̇·nēz
Theseus   thē′sūs
Thrasea   thrā′sė̇·a
Tiberius   tī·bėr′ĭ·ŭs
Troezen   trē′zĕn

NOTE: In "Pasiphaë" the final e is long; everywhere else, as in "Andromache," "Oenone," etc., it has a very short "ee" sound, not really distinguishable from short *i*. The *eus* ending, as in "Theseus," is spoken in one syllable, rhyming with "deuce." The *es* ending, as in "Orestes," "Pylades," "Theramenes," etc., is invariably "eez." There are four syllables in "Pirithous."

[1] Webster's symbols.